Praise for
We Should Do This More Often

"What a challenge! Sexual intimacy in a marriage with young children! Lorilee Craker motivates us to make it happen."
— ELISA MORGAN, president and CEO, MOPS
International (Mothers of Preschoolers)

"My husband highly recommends *We Should Do This More Often.* Maybe it was throwing away my ratty nightshirt and replacing it with something a bit more, well, racy, that won him over. Or perhaps it was the romantic CD I compiled for us to dance to while the kids spent the weekend at Grandma's. He didn't really say. All he knows is, ever since his wife read Lorilee Craker's sassy call to reclaim prechild marital fun, things have been a bit more *interesting* around the home front—and yes, the bedroom. Ladies, grab this book! You and your hubby will be glad you did."
— JULIE ANN BARNHILL, author of *Radical Forgiveness,*
Scandalous Grace, 'Til Debt Do Us Part, and the
bestseller *She's Gonna Blow!*

"Lorilee has written a hilarious and true description of romance-deprived marriage. *We Should Do This More Often* is a must-read for couples."
— SHONNA SMITH, star of the A&E reality series
Family Plots

"I love this book. It's funny, and I related to so many of the women in Lorilee's stories. I loved it most of all because it reassured me that the pleasure of intimacy with my husband is one of the best things I can do for the strength of my family."

—CINDY MORGAN, wife, mother, singer, and songwriter

"This terrific book is for anyone who's ever thought, *Sleep or sex? Well duh!* Lorilee's latest guide for moms reminds us that sex is as important as sleep in a marriage—and can be just as comforting and relaxing. Not to mention fun! Her light style takes the drudgery out and shows off all the enjoyment of rekindling the fire with your husband."

—DR. KEVIN LEMAN, author of *Sheet Music*

We Should Do
THIS
More Often

We Should Do THIS More Often

A Parents' Guide to Romance,
Passion, and Other
Prechild Activities You Vaguely Recall

LORILEE CRAKER

WATERBROOK
PRESS

WE SHOULD DO THIS MORE OFTEN
PUBLISHED BY WATERBROOK PRESS
2375 Telstar Drive, Suite 160
Colorado Springs, Colorado 80920
A division of Random House, Inc.

The author of this book is not a physician, and the ideas, procedures, and suggestions in this book are not intended as a substitute for the medical advice of a trained health professional. All matters regarding your health require medical supervision. Consult your physician before adopting the suggestions in this book, as well as about any condition that may require diagnosis or medical attention. The author and publisher disclaim any liability arising directly or indirectly from the use of the book.

All Scripture quotations, unless otherwise indicated, are taken from the *New American Standard Bible®*. © Copyright The Lockman Foundation 1960, 1962, 1963, 1968, 1971, 1972, 1973, 1975, 1977, 1995. Used by permission. (www.Lockman.org.) Scripture quotations marked (KJV) are taken from the *King James Version.*

Details in some anecdotes and stories have been changed to protect the identities of the persons involved.

ISBN 1-57856-859-5

Published in association with the literary agency of Alive Communications, Inc., 7680 Goddard Street, Suite 200, Colorado Springs, CO 80920.

Library of Congress Cataloging-in-Publication Data
Craker, Lorilee.
    We should do this more often : a parents' guide to romance, passion, and other prechild activities you vaguely recall / Lorilee Craker.— 1st ed.
        p. cm.
    Includes bibliographical references.
    ISBN 1-57856-859-5
    1. Sex—Religious aspects—Christianity. 2. Marriage—Religious aspects—Christianity.
3. Christian women—Religious life. I. Title.
    BT708.C73 2005
    613.9'6'085—dc22   2004022769

Printed in the United States of America
2005—First Edition

10 9 8 7 6 5 4 3 2 1

To Buck, I love you.

—Verna Jayne

My beloved is mine, and I am his.

Song of Solomon 2:16

Contents

Contents

Acknowledgments

To Doyle, first and foremost, for helping me with "research" for this book; for being a great, helpful husband and father; and for allowing me to divulge so much personal info about you. (You come off like a major stud, just so you know!)

To Jonah and Ezra, for giving Mom and Dad two big excuses to revamp our love lives! May you two always put your wives first some day, and may you enjoy a lifetime of passion the way God designed you to.

To my parents, Abe and Linda Reimer, for continued support and prayer.

To my hilarious, wonderful girlfriends, who dished many stories from your own love shacks for this book. Since many of your names have been changed, I won't reveal them now. You know who you are.

To experts, such as Kevin Leman, Karen Linamen, the Berman sisters, Michelle Wiener-Davis, Ellen Kreidman, and especially Valerie Davis Raskin, for your wealth of knowledge and insight on the topic of sexuality.

To Oprah Winfrey, for your amazingly dead-on "Getting in Touch with Your Inner Sexpot" episode. It sparked this whole book!

The Madison Square Church MOPS group: uh huh... Thanks for all the giggles, girls, not to mention for filling out my little questionnaires. We all know way too much about one another.

To my essential and fabulous Writer's Guild ladies who encourage me, prop me up after disappointments, tell me I'm amazing when I feel anything but, and the list goes on and on... Ann Byle, Tracy Groot, Jen Abbas, and Julie Johnson. I love you, girls.

Other writer friends, who are so marvelous and cool and inspiring: Julie Barnhill, Beth Lagerborg, Laura Jensen Walker, and Lisa Tawn Bergren. I aspire to be like you guys.

To my agent, Chip MacGregor: you're a great buddy and a terrific, encouraging agent-man, but you dance way too fast for your own good.

To Bob Wood and Pat Chown, my Canuck connections: thanks for ads in Canadian flyers, for keeping me plugged in to the True North, and for Blue Jays tix. I am so thankful for you both.

To the WaterBrook family, especially Don Pape and Laura Barker, for believing in me and my writing, for caring about my life and my family, and for all the tender, loving care you put into each book.

To Laura Wright, for carefully catching my right-brained "misses," all with a wry smile and a cool sense of humor. I'm definitely taking you up on your invite to come to NYC!

And finally, to Erin Healy, a dream to do a book with, who has spoiled me for any and all future editors. For reading my mind, knowing my heart, getting my weird sense of humor, boosting my spirits, and being my friend as well as my editor—thank you, thank you, thank you. I hope we always stay connected.

We Should Do
THIS
More Often

Before There Were Bunnies

To say one's sex life changes after becoming a parent is like saying the prairies look a bit disheveled after a tornado. It's the understatement of the century. The happy interludes of young married couple life fly out the door the minute that swaddled bundle of joy is carried in. (Of course, the first and third trimesters of pregnancy should have served as big clues that the fun and frolic of prebaby days were about to morph into something else entirely, but I digress.)

Babies always choose to yell their head off at exactly the wrong moment. Even if they snooze on cue—no small feat, of course—new parents are way too zonked to consider engaging in the activity that got them into this situation in the first place. Sleep or sex? Well, duh.

Toddlers sleep through the night, one would hope, but they do have the ability to clamber out of their cribs or toddler beds and make their way to Mommy and Daddy's chambers—with little regard for privacy or timing.

Preschoolers are even worse because they want to know what in the Sam Hill is going on in there. If the child is any older, a *kiddus interruptus* is an occasion for severe and indelibly imprinted mortification on both sides. Just ask my mother-in-law or my husband (at different times, please).

No doubt about it, sex loses some serious snap, crackle, and pop once the kiddies arrive on the scene. For many parents, the pitter-patter of little feet is a death knell that tolls for their passionate love life. Fear of getting caught in the act, plus the constant energy drain of parenting, is water enough to douse even the hottest of sexual fires. As a result, even parents who were once highly compatible lovers often see their sex life fizzle. Because a healthy sex life is integral to a happy marriage, this "loss of lust" can become a major disruption in a couple's relationship.

"The birth of each child signals a serious and permanent alteration in your marriage," write Drs. Les and Leslie Parrott, codirectors of the Center for Relationship Development at Seattle Pacific University. "Studies show that when Baby makes three, conflicts increase eightfold: marriage takes a backseat; women feel overburdened and men feel shoved aside. By the baby's first birthday, most mothers are less happy about their marriage, and some are wondering whether their marriage will even make it. Baby-induced marital meltdowns are not uncommon."[1]

In a poll taken by *Parents* magazine, 87 percent of moms admitted they don't make love as often as they did before having kids, and a third confessed their love life has taken a "major nose-dive" since the advent of Baby. (Eighteen percent actually said sex was the same, exactly the same, as before they became parents, but they must have clicked the wrong button or something. Something.)[2]

❀ Two Who Used to Tango

I would like to introduce you to Trevor and Debra Arbuckle, a mutually adoring couple whose love life is about to experience a major bump in the road. Throughout the pages of this book, we'll peek through the keyhole of their bedroom door and glimpse what happens to a marriage when a family begins to grow.

But first a little note about the whole Trevor-and-Debra saga and why I chose to weave their story throughout these pages. Many women told me their stories for this book, sharing openly how they struggled with sexual intimacy after their kids were born. They also gave me great insights and tips to pass along on how they eventually tapped into their inner Red-Hot Mama and got back in touch with that part of their married self. Several people asked me to change their names or mix up the details to hide their identity.

So I decided to cobble all their stories in a way that highlighted the big themes of this book.

The result is the tale of a fictional couple who gradually find their way back to passion. It's a simplistic and general story, but since this isn't a full-length novel (or a novel, period), it had to be that way. Their circumstances reflect the nitty-gritty of what it means to be married with children and how the very blessing of kids can wreak havoc on a romantic relationship. Trevor and Debra are one small part imagination, one large part real life, and a dash of me and my husband, Doyle. I brought family members, like parents and siblings, into their story because our key relationships affect who we are and how we deal with our changing lives. The skinny sister? She belongs to one of my good friends. Trevor's sister Laura? Okay, she's pretty much me—an idealized version anyway. And that's all you get on true identities in this little saga of sex lost and regained. Wild horses couldn't drag the rest from me!

So gather round the keyhole here. We first encounter the young lovers in the heady, prechild, salad days of their union, when everything was still humming along quite nicely in the nooky department.

❀ TREVOR AND DEBRA, PART 1: THE HAPPY RABBIT STAGE

Before they had Baby Number One, Trevor and Debra were like a couple of overheated rabbits, according to how they remember it.

In the years before they became parents, they couldn't keep their hands off each other. Trevor was in husband heaven with Debra, and because of their wildly passionate sex life, he felt very close to his wife. While their married friends would sometimes take each other for granted, Trevor tried to be in tune with Debra's needs in and out of the bedroom. He knew she loved to cuddle while watching movies at home, and he was so crazy about her he willingly provided all the affection she needed.

Deb was mad about Trevor too. She hadn't had any real sexual experience before they got married, but she happened to think her guy was the world's best lover. At work, Debra would sometimes smile to herself as she thought about their fantastic lovemaking the night before. She wasn't shy about bringing home magazine articles about sex and asking Trevor if he would mind "trying it out" with her. If ever there was a rhetorical question…

As a couple, Trevor and Debra were the envy of their social group. The Arbuckles were friends, lovers, and soul mates. Trevor's buddies would sometimes tease him: "Hey, Trevor, just wait until you have kids!" Naturally, he never believed them. A baby, he knew, would only add to their feelings of love and affection for each other.

Ah, there's nothing like a little prechild honeymoon bliss to make the rest of us gape in wonder, awe, and—yeah—jealousy. Are these guys in la-la land or what? Totally. Of course, upon the momentous birth of their firstborn child—make that about six weeks later—enter the sound of screeching breaks; camera pans to shocked couple. Who knew passion could take such a nosedive?

I'm guessing that you do, because why else would you be reading this book?

Sex can be one of the most fabulous things two people can do together. It can excite us, energize us, relax us, soothe our souls, relieve our stress, and reconnect us with each other. Why, then, do so many of us parents put sex at the bottom of our priority list?

With the little folk to chase, bathe, clothe, feed, entertain, and corral, have we become too busy to enjoy this gratifying diversion? Or are we so totally frazzled that we don't even recognize the pure enjoyment good sex can provide? Look, we're not talking about bunion surgery here. We're talking about bliss, fire, wahoo!

Because two decades is a long time to go without passion, *We Should Do This More Often* talks up the importance of sex for one's health, for one's sanity, and, of course, for a thriving, percolating marriage. It may seem like the least important thing in the world, what with colicky babies, teething toddlers, and demanding preschoolers, but sex is paramount to nurturing the bond between Mom and Dad. This means it can only be good for the kids, too.

Parenthood doesn't have to put a dent in your sex life—or even a crimp. Get this: Some moms report even more excitement and satisfaction with the main man between the sheets. I'm not naming names or anything. I'm just saying they're out there and they're willing to talk.

In a way it makes sense. Making love used to be a no-brainer—an anytime, anyplace activity where fun was (usually) had by all. Throw kids into the mix, and *amoré* becomes loaded with obstacles. But when you meet the challenges with creativity, determination, and teamwork—and you gotta have teamwork!—the rewards can be that much sweeter.

ONE

What's the Big Whoop?

Why Sex Matters to a Marriage

H ey, it's just fifteen minutes out of your life," my friend Emily quipped about sex. "Twenty if you're lucky." Because most young parents have sex about once a week on average, we can do the math: Sex really shouldn't take up more than an hour or two a month, tops. So what's the big whoop about it? Why is the act of passion so vitally important to the foundations of marriage and family life? Is it really that important?

Actually, yes! Romance and intimacy are marriage musts— *especially* when the pitter-patter of little feet can be heard. With each child who comes along, Mom and Dad's relationship is that much more squeezed for time and energy. Gradually, the couple who started the family can easily drift apart.

Being lovers is a big deal. Romance, passion—good old-fashioned nooky—can be the glue that holds two people together. Sex is about much more than mere physical pleasure. It's about mutual connection, intimacy, closeness, and affection. It's about feeling attractive, feeling masculine/feminine, and feeling whole as a person. It's about being in love. It's about sharing a feeling of oneness.

Couples who enjoy great sex report a higher quality of life, and they experience less depression. Regular action between the sheets is the perfect buffer for the stress in our lives—it helps us stay healthy and happy. In other words, husbands and wives who make their sexual relationship a priority feel good about themselves and about life in general. "In relationships where [passion] is lacking, things just don't feel quite right," says marriage therapist Susan Hubbard. "It's like trying to drive a car with only three wheels. A car that cruises on all four tires is more likely to go the distance, especially over rocky roads."[1]

Many, many couples drive through their married lives with a missing wheel. If you feel as if the sizzle in your relationship is a bit off balance, you're not alone. Studies show one out of every three couples struggles with problems associated with low sexual desire. One study found that 20 percent of married couples have sex less than ten times a year! In fact, low desire is the number one problem brought to sex therapists.[2]

As you look for ways to keep that fourth tire securely attached to your marriage vehicle, keep in mind three reasons why cultivating passion is such a big deal:

1. YOUR CHILDREN WILL BENEFIT

Tammy and Dwight were kissing in the kitchen, and their fifteen-year-old son regarded them with alarm. "Do you have to do that when I'm around?" he asked incredulously. "They say kids are supposed to feel more secure when their parents make out," Tammy said. "It means your parents' marriage is not on the rocks." Eric rolled his eyes. "Can't you just shake hands or something?"

As a teenager, of course, Eric thinks his parents' affection is gross. Can't you remember wincing at your mom and dad when they started smooching in the kitchen—or anywhere? Actually, if you do recall catching your parents canoodling, you're one of the lucky ones because chances are good that they're still together and probably happy.

Your marriage is the backbone of your family. It needs to stay strong in order for the kids to be happy and healthy and to ensure the longevity and sturdiness of your tribe. Long after your kids are grown and gone, you two will be together. Some people justify their lack of interest in postbaby romance by saying, "When the kids are gone, we can find our way back to each other again." Maybe. But wouldn't it be a far better plan to retool your love life

11

now, so your kids can know the happiness and stability of growing up in a home with loving parents? And, because you are their primary sexual role models, your vibrant romance will help your kids define healthy sexual identities of their own.

Psychologist Kevin Leman tells the story of a couple who planned and accomplished a hot little rendezvous one day at their home. The kids? They were parked at Grandma's. "When Jim and Karen finally picked up the younger kids from Grandma's house, Jim couldn't wait to see them. Because he was sexually satisfied, he could focus fully on being there for his kids, hearing about their day, and taking time to tuck them into bed. And don't think the kids didn't notice how affectionate Jim and Karen were that evening. It gave them a sense of security and happiness, making them think, *We're in the best family anyone could be in.*"[3]

2. YOUR MARRIAGE WILL BENEFIT

One of the first red flags in a passionless marriage is that the husband and wife aren't affectionate. They stop holding hands, hugging, and cuddling even behind closed doors. The reason for this? Sometimes men stop being affectionate because they're unfulfilled to begin with, and they don't want to get something going that will ultimately never come to pass. Others think that giving their wife a little pat on the behind might be taken to mean they're trying to seduce her, at which point she'll shut them down. Women, meanwhile, might not grab their partner's hand or rub his shoulders because they fret about how their intentions will look. Will he take her hug to mean she's in the mood for more, even when she's just in the mood for a hug, and that's it? Couples will go round and round to avoid possible rejection.

On the other hand, sexy duos like each other, and they aren't afraid to show it. They kiss, cuddle, hold hands, flirt, and carry on until onlookers want to tell them to get a room. Even undemonstrative people, when embroiled in a hot, married love affair, are kind and smiling and attentive to their lovers.

Quotable

"Marriage and all that comes with it is a huge vote of confidence in the future. So we flowed forward. A year after we married, we bought a house. Then we had Luke. There wasn't much time to do the things we did when we were falling in love—the long runs together, the Sunday afternoon reading sessions with our legs entwined—but there was new stuff. Raising our son together gave me a sense of partnership that I'd never felt in my life. Things seemed limitless, and Anne so lovely."

—Stephen Madden[4]

Now sex doesn't make or break a marriage, but it matters—a lot. It can deepen and toughen your bond and reduce the stress that comes with sharing a life, the kids, a dog, and a mortgage. It's true that sex is just one component of your relationship, but it's a biggie. If it's messed up, chances are good that other aspects of your union are wobbly too. But if you and your mate engage in regular hanky-panky, you will just plain get along better. Research supports the idea that spouses who revel in romance between the sheets are more cheerful, less demanding, less irritable, and more willing to go the extra mile for one another.

Marriage therapist Michele Weiner-Davis, author of *The Sex-Starved Marriage,* names these personal payoffs of shoring up your marital sex life:

> When you show your caring…by making sex a bigger priority in your marriage, she/he will appreciate your efforts and become more caring toward you. You will see it in his or her eyes. You'll start getting love notes and witness random acts of kindness. Your spouse will begin to open up and be decidedly more interested in you as a person. He'll stop what he's doing to hear about something you find interesting on television. She will notice your strengths rather than criticize. He will agree to go shopping with you at the mall. She'll give her blessings to that boys' night out for which you've been hankering. In short, a miracle will happen. It will take you back to the times in your relationship when everything was clicking.[5]

Now, let me just be crystal clear: If your marriage is gasping for breath, regular sex alone is not going to get it breathing on its own again. Counseling is in order if you fear things between you and your husband are falling apart. If you have a foundationally sound union, though, with the normal problems and sticking points that plague every marriage, perking up your sex life could be the tonic that infuses your relationship with the goods to make it great.

3. GOD WANTS YOU TO HAVE A THRILLING SEX LIFE

He really does. Throw away your notions of a God tsk-tsking in the heavenly realm, a disapproving school principal who can't wait to give you detention for getting it on. When you're married, He says, "Go for it! Have fun, kids." In his book *Sacred Sex,* counselor Tim Alan Gardner writes: "God could have arranged the whole reproduction thing any way he wanted: a hidden button, a super secret handshake, or some unique facial exchange that brought about conception. Really, he could have. But instead he designed sex."[6]

There's no escaping it: God made you and your mate sexual beings, hard-wired with a craving to be intimate and to experience pleasure. "Since the creation of male and female, sex was to be the way that a husband and wife were to touch each other's soul," Dr. Gardner writes.

A couple of Bible-time hotties, Solomon and his lover Shulamith, certainly touched each other's souls—and a whole lotta other places. If you've never cracked open the Song of Solomon, the steamiest book of the Old Testament, or if you've never gotten past the whole "your hair is like a flock of goats" thing, peel back Sol and Shuli's tent flap again and prepare to be amazed.

Did you know that the word *garden* is a poetic term for *vagina* in the Song and that *fruit* is actually a cheeky little name for the male package? Keeping this in mind, check out these white-hot passages: "In his shade I took great delight and sat down, and his fruit was sweet to my taste" (2:3). And, "Awake, O north wind; and come, thou south; blow upon my garden, that the spices thereof may flow out" (4:16, KJV). You go, sister Shulamith!

In their invaluable book *Intimate Issues,* Linda Dillow and Lorraine Pintus explore the most erotic book of the Bible and unearth some rather erotic tips for lovers throughout the ages. Apparently Shulamith and Solomon employed the use of fragrant oils, incense, and powders to stimulate the potent sense of smell. They got each other all hot and bothered with their mutual admiration—"your two breasts are like two fawns" (4:5)—and they were not in the least bit stingy when it came to complimenting each other's skills in the sack. And get this: belly dancing is endorsed by God! "Commentators agree that 'the curves of your hips' (7:1) refer to their swaying motion as she dances before Solomon," write Dillow and Pintus. "God designed the male mind (and other parts of his body) to respond to visual images. Shulamith filled her husband's eyes with images that sent him into ecstasy."[7]

Reread the Song of Solomon with these things in mind, and see if this doesn't send you to belly-dancing class or at least to the market for pomegranates!

FROM BIG WHOOP TO BIG WHOOPEE

Has your sex life grown stale? Do you feel as if you've become almost asexual in the trenches of raising your kids? Like anything worthwhile, reviving sexual energy in your marriage will take some work, but it can be done. "Sex is critically important for a quality marriage," say the Parrotts. "What most couples don't understand is how an intentional effort can keep the flames of passion burning strong—even between changing diapers and making formula."[8]

With intentional effort, you can hit upon new ways to keep your romantic energy alive. With intentional effort, you can discover ways to reinvent the sexual side of your relationship with your husband. You can keep track of the challenges to your love life, the obstacles presented by your body, the ups and downs of your relationships, and the libido busters of the daily grind. When you're more aware of the hurdles, you can better jump them.

With intentional effort, you can find your inner Red-Hot Mama. You can reclaim your previous luscious self. Trust me—she's in there! Now let's get busy, girls, and find her.

TWO

Baby Is Not the King Around Here

How to Take the Tyranny Out of Your Child-Centered Family

When Debra gave birth to Avery, she and Trevor were both instantly smitten to the core with their beautiful new baby. Trevor would tell anyone who would listen that Avery was "Daddy's girl." But the truth was that he hardly ever got to hold her, never mind bathe or feed her. Debra had quit her job to take care of the baby full time. Trevor supported this decision, even though money was tight, but when he would get home, eager to spend time with his wife and child, and maybe even give Debra a break, he felt like an outsider in his own family.

As full-time caregiver, Debra was laser-focused on Avery. As an exclusive breast-feeder, she handled the entire feeding aspect of Avery's care. When Trevor suggested that Debra pump milk into a bottle so he could take some of the feedings, or even alternate sometimes with formula, she responded with indignation. She wanted to be the one to supply nourishment to Avery. End of story.

That was one thing, Trevor thought, but why couldn't he, as a competent adult, bond with his daughter by bathing her or changing her diaper?

When Avery napped, Debra was in the mood for sleep. Noth-

Burn, Baby, Burn

Got a CD burner? Surprise your husband with a "burning" disc filled with songs that help you express how much you want him and what you wish to do with him when you two next hit the sheets. I'm not talking a CD for family listening here! Pick songs that suit your tastes, put words to your most intimate feelings, and get your hubby thinking of you (regardless of what the songwriters might have originally intended). In other words, make your collection personal and passionate. Don't know where to begin? Maybe these will spark some ideas:

ing else. Any overtures Trevor made for romance were met with rolled eyes and, "Yeah right." Trevor couldn't figure out how his formerly passionate mate had become so indifferent. Six months had passed since Avery's birth, and very little had returned to normal.

WHEN IT'S ALL ABOUT THE KIDS

For many couples, raising kids becomes not just one aspect of marriage but its entire intent and focus. The husband or wife—and sometimes both—views the other mainly as copresident of Kid Care Co., not as a romantic and sexual companion. When that happens, says writer Caitlin Flanagan, "All of domestic life now

---

"Love Me As Though There Were No Tomorrow" (Nat King Cole)

"Touch" (Amy Grant)

"I Want You to Want Me" (Cheap Trick)

"Give Me a Kiss to Build a Dream On" (Louis Armstrong)

"Our Little World" (Susan Ashton)

"Possession" (Sarah MacLachlan)

"Endless Love" (Lionel Richie and Diana Ross)

"Open Arms" (Journey)

"As Time Goes By" (Jimmy Durante)

"More Than Words" (Extreme)

"Recipe for Love" (Harry Connick Jr.)

---

turns on the entertainment and happiness not of the adults but of the children."[1]

It's all too easy to get wrapped up in the world of parenting, where we are on call 24-7 to apply Band-Aids, dispense Popsicles, monitor television viewing, and clean up gallons of spilled milk. The care and feeding of children is so labor intensive, in fact, that a mother might wonder what she did with all those free hours before she had kids.

Couples tend to underestimate just how much of their free time evaporates after they have kids," writer Johnathon Allen says.

> Enjoying sex is a lot like eating a gourmet meal, and sufficient preparation time is essential for both. As a result, plenty of casually interactive time is a crucial nutrient for sustaining lively libidos. Without it, couples don't have the space they need to develop their inner passions. This is especially true for women. A man may be content with a ten-minute microwave dinner, but women need to feel like they have time to let the ingredients simmer. They like to have a few appetizers and feel pampered. So, whether sex is part of the plan or not, it's important that parents create time when they know they'll have a baby-sitter, or can be together for an afternoon, so they have room to naturally advance the romance in their relationship.[2]

For first-time parents like Debra, this is especially true. Moms want to do their very best, which, in a popular yet flawed line of thinking, means never leaving their precious babies for an instant, not even to spend time with the old sperm donor (er, father). Experts say that many of us overfeed the children and starve the marriage. I've seen this dynamic play out again and again. A couple will have their first baby. Naturally, Ma and Pa are gaga over the child, attending to her every need with an enormous amount of attention and devotion. This is as it should be! But somehow along the way, many moms tend to coast unknowingly into a realm where Baby is king, not prince, and the former love of their life becomes chief bottle washer, diaper fetcher, bill payer, and—let's face it—roommate.

Is anything easier than sliding into a pattern of putting our kids before their dad? It's so simple that a surprising number of moms do so without even realizing it. A child needs to be fed, changed, dressed, rocked... His needs are never-ending, and he's so helpless. After all, your guy is a grown man, totally capable of taking care of himself. But the little ones need Mom to do just about everything for them. Or do they? Kids require that we meet their basic needs of being fed, clothed, loved, and set on the right path, but one of the main things they need is for Mom and Dad to love each other and build a strong relationship with each other. This they need infinitely more than they need your being home every night of the week catering to their every whim.

Let me repeat something here for emphasis: "Plenty of casually interactive time is a crucial nutrient for sustaining lively libidos," Allen says. "Without it, couples don't have the space they need to develop their inner passions." Oh, that I could shout those words from the rooftops! We absolutely must make the time and create the space to fan the flames of romance, or we will become passionless, cardboard replicas of the women we once were. What a tragedy that would be!

Michele Weiner-Davis is convinced that the biggest breakdown factor in today's relationships is that couples don't spend enough time together. "And when relationships aren't attended to as they should be," she says, "trouble sets in."[3] I couldn't agree more with Weiner-Davis's evaluation. I am amazed by parents who neglect their mates but would walk a mile over hot coals for their children. I also see couples who, after meeting their kids' needs, pour any leftover energies they may have into doing their own thing, whether it be fishing, golfing, scrapbooking, or shopping. Don't get me wrong: We need to carve out time and space for the activities we love, but not at the expense of our mates. It's so easy to give and give and give to our kids, eke out a little time for ourselves, and have precious little—if anything at all—left for the one we married. Then we wake up one day and realize we don't even know the guy who's snoring next to us, never mind want to engage in wild passion with him!

More and more, experts are underscoring the importance of

couplehood as the foundation of parenthood. If you don't plan dates anymore because you fear your kids will feel neglected, remember what I mentioned in chapter 1: As long as your kids' basic needs are being met, the children will actually feel happy and secure knowing that their parents have a loving, connected relationship. "Taking care of your couple relationship *is* taking care of your kids," says therapist Carole-Anne Vatcher in an article called "When Parenting Threatens Your Couple Relationship." "The couple relationship is the backbone of the nuclear family. It needs to stay strong in order for the kids to be happy and healthy, and to ensure the longevity and sturdiness of the family."[4]

For those of you who are still sputtering, "But, but, but…," here's one more thing to consider: If you consistently fuel your partnership and turn to your main man for love and nurturing, you will parent your kids from a full tank. A *full* tank, sister-friend! But if you undervalue your marriage for too long, you risk running on fumes.

THE DISH: "SHE'S NOT THE ONLY ONE TO GET KISSES!"

The moms I interviewed for this book talked up many subjects that will appear throughout these pages. For starters, their candid confessions in response to this question: who comes first—the man who used to make your knees weak or his offspring?

"Yes, I definitely think my husband gets pushed to the back

burner now that we have two girls," Mary admitted. "But who doesn't push her husband to the side, at least some of the time? Besides, most of the time the girls are so much cuter than he is." Ouch! That's got to smart a little for Mary's husband—to hear his wife say that he just doesn't cut it in the cuteness department. But I think Mary is being honest.

"I don't think I 'starve the marriage,'" Johana said, "but I do tend to put the kids' needs and house cleanliness or bills over having an intimate night. Jonathan will sometimes point this out in arguments. He'll say he is my last priority, and I get mad because I think I put myself as last priority. I know our marriage needs to be first, so that's the sad part."

Erika, a first-time mom of twin toddlers, realizes how easy it is to skate right into the kids-first mode. "Since our babies are only one year old, they're just now getting beyond that intense stage of us simply providing for their basic needs," she said. "Up until now, yeah, our tendency has been to be overwhelmed by the demands of our two little ones, but already I can tell that it's lightening up. Hopefully we'll be able to find a healthy balance. But I can see the dangers of slipping into focusing on the kids at the expense of our marriage."

Leave it to my pal Amy Q., mom of five, to nail it: "I think we [starved our marriage and overfed the kids] at first, but we are realizing that kids will always try to demand more of our time, so we need to show them that our love and commitment to each other comes first. The best gift we can give to our kids is time spent keeping our marriage strong. Then hopefully the rest of the family will follow." You said it, Amy! Kids will demand as much as they can get away with demanding. It's up to us as the mature parental units to set loving limits that leave lots of room for Ma and Pa's love life to grow!

And, finally, let's hear from Emily, an old soul in a twenty-something body. She's wise enough to know that George, the love of her life, should come first: "Before we had Vera, we had many discussions about the expectations we had for our relationship postkids. The greatest gift we can give Vera is a healthy example of two people who love being together and who show it. We make an effort to be affectionate with each other around her, so she knows she's not the only one to get kisses around here!"

Mojo Makeover: Take Back Your Marriage

If little usurpers have overtaken your relationship with your husband, the first order of the day will be to topple their tyrannical regime and reassume your rightful place as king and queen of the family domain. How do you do that? A great first step to insist on making time for each other. Be awake to the fact that your kids don't want you to spend time on your marriage. They have no idea, of course, that your strong and sexy union is in their best interest. All they know is that they want you around to dote on them and cater to their every whim. But children can learn to respect their parents' time, so insist on devoting a generous portion of that time to your spouse. The kids will survive. I promise.

Find the Off Switch

Remember David Letterman teasing his mom by mimicking her constant, "I do, and do, and doooo for you kids"? If you believe that being a "good" mother means you have to do for your kids until you've exhausted every smidgen of your energy, no wonder you're too tired for romance. "Maternal perfectionism and excessive self-sacrifice is a treadmill with no off switch," says physician Valerie Davis Raskin.[5] Turn that treadmill off! Exploring the best way to do that is another book entirely, so for those who need help with this, I'll recommend these good titles that other moms in the know have already written: *Time Out for Mom...Ahhh Moments* (Zondervan, 2000) by Cynthia Sumner and *The Mother Load* by Mary Byers (Harvest House, 2005).

Get Out of Mommy Zone and into Lovers' Lane

"John came up with a decorating technique to help us get out of the parenting mode," Marisol said. "He'll bring down blankets and comforters and will make a 'bed' for us on the floor. Then we'll watch a romantic movie. Sometimes it'll lead to something. Other times it won't. For me, knowing that it doesn't have to lead to something has actually enabled me to initiate more, which he likes."

My friend Annie also found a way to switch gears between mother and lover: "I have Dan take over bedtime duties while I take some time for myself to read a book, usually something funny or escapist," she said. "Or I take a bath and maybe even shave my legs or paint my toenails. After a day of a toddler using me for a Kleenex, a bath and a little nail polish does quite a bit to restore feelings of femininity!" Amen!

"We had to consciously look for ideas to inspire our couple-dom and serve as a palate cleanser between our mommy/daddy roles and our private, amorous relationship," wrote Joan K. Peters in an article titled "Showing Our Love." "Being lovers at home, in our daily lives, was crucial. To our dinners and our after-dinner strolls we added the weekend massage: we'd deck our room out with candles, Tibetan elevator music, and fragrant oils to create a homemade spa. Little by little, we tunneled our way back to each other as a couple."[6]

Support Each Other's Parenting

Do we ever get enough pats on the back for a mommy job well done? Probably not. Do we give out the kind of strokes we are looking for from our mates? Again, probably not! And friction over child-rearing matters can place a real strain on your romantic feelings. Who feels like being sexual when she's just heard Dad tell the kids, "No, you don't have to do what Mom says"?

Make parenting part of your closeness as a couple by recognizing and praising your husband for the good job he's doing. Ask him to do the same. You two are a team, and the more you function as partners, cheering each other on as you raise the kids you both adore, the more effectively you'll develop an "us" and "them" mentality. You two are the coaches, and the munchkins are the squad. Just make sure that as coaches you hit the "bench" often!

Commit Random Acts of Kindness

Try whipping up his favorite dessert and surprising him if he's been having a rough week at the office. Or bring him Chinese takeout if he's stuck at work.

It'll take you two minutes to make his day. Simply put, it's the little things that keep him remembering what an amazing woman he married. Not only that, tiny courtesies can be contagious.

Get Out of Your Platonic Rut

Go to bed together, kiss each other goodnight, and hop in the shower in your birthday suits as often as possible. Duh? Well, then do it! "It's the little things" also applies to lighting the romantic fires. So why not hit the sack together if you are both going to be reading for an hour? Going to bed together invites physical contact, such as cuddling, and cozy pillow talk. Smooches at bedtime need not lead to anything more steamy, but they send the message that, yes, the man right there beside you, reading his fishing magazine, is, after all, the romantic lead in your life. Showering together is a wonderful reminder of the privileges of marital cohabitation, especially if we've fallen into a platonic rut with our spouses. "Sometimes I feel like my husband is a brother or a cousin," Alyssa admitted to me once. "I mean, I love him, but I also love my brother!" "Shower together tonight!" I urged her. "It will be a clear statement of the fact that your husband is *not* your brother because, for Pete's sake, he's naked!" Standing under the water together in nothing but skin is the perfect reminder that marriage is anything but platonic.

Leave the Premises

I develop this thought extensively in the next chapter, but escaping the house for an evening, a weekend, or even longer may be the answer to reclaiming your passion with your main man. "Couples who have a good intimate relationship, kids or no kids, have a passion continually explored in a close relationship," family therapist Claire Maisonneuve says. "You don't need gadgets and expensive hotels, although there's no doubt sometimes it is better to get away."[7] Your rendezvous might entail anything from a lunch out to three hours at a hotel (wahoo!) to an overnight minivacation.

Whatever you choose, it's crucial to *get away* as a twosome once in a while—away from the kids, away from the house, the dog, and the plants.

Mom, pry yourself away from your precious progeny from time to time and devote yourself completely to your husband. You'll be amazed at the dividends this pays in your marriage and family. If this doesn't come easy, chapter 3 is for you.

❦ It Only Takes a Flirt to Get a Fire Going

Remember those heady dating days when all you had to do was exchange glances with your beloved and your heart would drop into your stomach? Remember how an accidental brush of your hands while taking a stroll would send an electric shock through you to your toes? Back then, a pat on the rear, a wink, or even a cheeky little compliment could make you both feel like a million bucks. And why not? You were flirting, like mad probably, so of course you felt amazing—and so did he. Those were the days, weren't they? The highly charged days! Wouldn't it be incredible to regain some of that electricity?

Listen, I've been married for almost thirteen years now, and I know all too well that I never feel weak in the knees anymore—unless I have the flu. But I do believe it's possible to create romantic crackle in any marriage no matter how long you've been hitched or how many pairs of men's underwear you've folded. Your flirting moves may be a little rusty at this point, but it's never too late to trot them out again.

Listen to Tera's firsthand account of how a well-placed flirt here and there set off sparks in her marriage:

> Several months ago I was having a hard time really committing to [our love life]. I was too tired, my husband's father had just passed away, work was stressful, my son started school, I had a hangnail, and so on. Not much was going on in our bedroom except sleep. We'd been down this dark path several years before, and it had gotten really bad. I determined that I would *not* allow that to happen again. So, I started flirting. Not with the mailman, or the guy I work with, or the pizza delivery boy, but with my husband. I realized that what we were lacking was spark. Pizzazz. Spontaneous combustion. When I thought about what had happened when we first began dating many moons ago, I realized that what was missing was the flirting game. The teasing. The sideways glances. The patting of derrières. The quick peck on the cheek. The looooooong kiss in the hall. Know what? It worked. I became more turned on because he started flirting back. When you grab your spouse in the hall two hours before bedtime and smooch him a little… Well, let's just say I couldn't keep my hands off the guy!

Sparkplugs!

It's easy to forget just how yummy a night of passion can be. But it's not too late to get unstuck from your platonic ruts and bring intensity and physical excitement back into your marriage. Here for you is the first batch of flirty tips called "Sparkplugs," which I've sprinkled throughout this book and which have helped other moms spark once again the flash, the luster, the brilliance in their romantic lives. Try one on for size—hey, try them all!—and see if things don't become a whole lot "warmer" around the ol' hacienda. In this installment: cyberflirting.

- "I send my husband e-mails saying that I can't wait to be alone with him. When he gets home, we flirt until the kids go to bed. We also bet on everything—football games, the outcome of a show we're watching, anything. We bet for, well, favors! And every once in a while, I light candles in the bedroom before we go to bed." —Nicole

- "Since our twins were born a year and a half ago, my husband and I don't have much time for each other. One thing that we have discovered is e-mail. When we have a few minutes in our day, we'll e-mail each other about what we are feeling lusty about that day. Or, if it's a 'hands-off' kind of week, we talk about what we wish we could do, or we do a countdown to when we can finish the thought! This little habit gets us thinking about sex almost all day, so the pump, so to speak, is primed when nighttime comes." —Joanie

- "We are very gadgety people, so it's no surprise that we would use the latest technology to flirt with each other. E-mail? That's so last year! Now we send little forget-me-nots as text messages on each other's cell phones. I'll say, 'I was reading this article, and there's something I want to try later when Ben's in bed.' He'll shoot me one ASAP, saying, 'I cannot wait for that, loverdoll!' Or sometimes it's just, 'You look cute in that shade of blue' or 'I'm thinking of you and praying for an awesome day.' Honestly, this text-messaging thing has given us a new lease on our love life!" —Paulina

- "If my husband's on the Internet, I'll go over and give him a little back rub or a kiss on the cheek. Sometimes we'll joke about all the Viagra junk mail he gets, like, 'You don't need that, do you?' If I'm watering the plants, he'll come over and grab my backside playfully. Little things like that seem to build throughout the evening, and by the time we drop into bed, we're totally in the mood for more!" —Naomi

THREE

Get Out of My Dreams and into My Minivan

With Emphasis on "Get Out"

When Avery was about eighteen months old, her parents' fifth wedding anniversary approached. Trevor knew Deb would never leave the baby for the weekend; in all these months, Debra had refused to leave Avery. Now, Trevor could understand his wife's protective instincts—he felt incredibly protective of their daughter as well—but he didn't see why they couldn't step out for a few hours every couple of weeks and leave Avery with one of her two sets of doting grandparents who lived in town. His mother, who lived a mere seven blocks away, was a career pediatric nurse! Even so, Debra refused.

In an effort to make their anniversary special, however, Trevor lobbied hard for a dinner out. It was time, he figured, to start dating again, to try to get to know the mother of his child all over again. Actually, it was way past time.

Debra, on the other hand, felt as if she saw Trevor every day. Wasn't it selfish to leave Avery just to go out with someone she saw all the time anyway? Her sister-in-law Laura went out with her husband quite often and left their two small children with Trevor's mom. Once, Laura and Mark had even gone away for a four-day cruise. Four days! Privately, Debra felt that Laura and Mark overdid it with their getaways. She would never leave Avery like that!

At the same time, she missed her carefree life with Trevor. Deb felt disloyal to Avery even thinking that, but there it was. Sometimes Debra and Trevor would laugh at a private joke, and just for a minute they would find themselves on the same page. Those moments, Deb knew, were too infrequent.

You Need to Leave the Building Once in a While—Am I Right?

Depending on your age, you may or may not remember Billy Ocean's 1986 hit "Into My Car," where Billy wished aloud that the woman of his dreams would get out of the imaginary realm and into his real life. Yes, the tune's a bit skanky if you think about it too deeply, but the point—at least on the surface—applies to husbands and wives who dream about the way their mutual passion used to express itself.

Sometimes all it takes for your libido to perk up is to leave the building, tool off in the family automobile, and experience a change of scenery. The reverse is also true: if you never get out of the house without your munchkins in tow, your libido can suffer. Gary Weaver Li, a father of two from Portland, Oregon, concurs. "Ironically, after we had kids, one of the best things for our sex life was living near our in-laws because we had consistent child care," he says. "After we moved away, it became *much* harder to find quality time together, and the lack of casual time for going out for dinner or having long talks certainly had a negative impact on our intimacy."[1]

The first step toward having time together is deciding that your marriage is worth the effort and investment involved in leaving your kids once in a while. Many moms think they are bad mothers if they leave their kids. Duos who used to hit first-run movies once a weekend now catch flicks only on DVD. Pairs who once shared long, leisurely dinners out now always eat in. Lovers who couldn't wait to check out the bedsprings of great hotels and cozy bed-and-breakfasts now wouldn't dream of leaving their home overnight even if Grandma lives nearby. Why? Because movie theaters and restaurants and bed-and-breakfasts are not where the precious kid is—at home!

I'm not suggesting that you hit the town three nights after the little tyke comes home, and I'm all for creative ways to date at home after the kids are in bed, but let's be reasonable. Girls, I know what it's like to want to be with my baby and to miss him after only a couple of hours. I would even go out on a limb here and say it's a mite difficult to leave your baby much at all during his first few months of life. (Your first baby, that is. You second- and third-timers out there know what I'm talking about!) But after six months or so, if you and Dad haven't left the house together without the baby, it's time to go. Listen up because I'm only going to yell this once:

THE BEST MOMS LEAVE THEIR KIDS ONCE IN A WHILE
IN ORDER TO NURTURE THEIR MARRIAGES!

Sometimes it just takes a little forethought and a dash of ingenuity to pull off a date you will remember for years. In her book *Pillow Talk,* funny woman Karen Scalf Linamen recalls the date that helped her and her mate, Larry, begin to reconnect as a couple after the birth of their first baby:

> In the month or two after our baby was born, sex just didn't seem like a high priority to me. I was sore, I was exhausted, and I was completely emotionally sated by the new love in our lives. I was also just weeks removed from the trenches

of childbirth and wasn't too keen on doing anything that might reenlist me for another tour of duty.

Still, in some buried part of my psyche, I knew that sex remained important—for my husband and for me as well.

I called Biola University where my husband was, at that time, chairman of the business department. I got Larry's secretary on the phone and asked her to set up a lunch appointment for Larry with an imaginary prospective student and his parents. Then I asked her to block out the rest of his afternoon. I arranged for a baby-sitter, then phoned a local motel down the street and reserved a room, which I stocked with flowers, grapes, a bottle of sparkling apple cider, and even our swimsuits in case we felt like hitting the pool.

On the appointed day I picked up Larry at his office and told him—surprise!—that I was his real lunch date. I then drove him to a Chinese restaurant that just happened to be on the first floor of the motel that I had chosen. After we ordered, I suggested taking a walk around the motel gardens until our food arrived. On our way out, I slipped a note to the waiter, asking for lunch to be delivered to our room. Outside, I placed a room key in Larry's hand and then waited for him to pick his jaw up off the sidewalk.

No interruptions, no baby crying. No rush, which was important to me since I was still wary about making love for the first time after the rigors of childbirth. Our Chinese food was cold by the time we retrieved it from outside the door, and we never did make it to the pool. It cost me eighty bucks and took a week to plan. But what a celebration.[2]

I'm sure it was difficult for a first-time mom like Karen to leave her little one, even with a trustworthy caregiver. But her investment surely paid off in big dividends for both Mom and Dad, as well as the baby, because the Linamens' little afternoon delight fortified their marriage and thus their family.

✿ RESURRECTING THE ART OF DATING

If you're one of those people who think you can recapture romance while still in the presence of your children, well, I'll just tell you: you can't! Sure, maybe the two of you will exchange longing glances or sweet looks in a restaurant over the tousled heads of the tykes whose meat you're cutting, but your experience won't even come close to that of an uninterrupted, one-on-one conversation.

Listen to a couple of moms from the Parent Soup Web site who weighed in with their notions for happy date nights:

Parent Souper Deb wrote: "Sometimes it's to a nice restaurant where macaroni and cheese is not on the menu and they don't hand out crayons when we walk in. Other times it's for things as prosaic as picking up an herbicide to get rid of poison ivy or the big question of choosing the proper grass seed for the bald patch in the backyard. Sometimes it's a 'big' date like dinner and tickets to a live theater performance; other times it's sharing a 99-cent Coke and parking by the airport to watch planes landing while listening to the car stereo."[3]

Andrea adds: "We keep the spark alive by having 'mystery dates.' My husband will plan a date for us and not tell me anything about it other than what time to be ready. It can be anything from dinner at a nice restaurant to a show at the theatre or a picnic supper at the park. He always takes time to prepare something special, and I find that as I am getting dressed for the night, the anticipation and curiosity get the better of me, and I feel like we are in high school again."[4]

Andrea really tapped into something big here. She said date nights make her feel as if she and her husband are in high school again. What a feeling! As I discussed in chapter 2, it's hard to get in touch with your relationship as romantic partners when you are always, always in parent mode. And trust me, you are in parent mode when you're at home. Even if the kiddies are fast asleep, they can wake up at any moment and *poof!* There goes your romantic interlude. At home, you and your loved one will always be aware that you are not really alone together. Plus, their stuff is everywhere, a constant reminder of them and—even more distracting—your parental responsibilities. Experts actually say that our house is often the worst place to find romance because of all the distractions there.

Some people really enjoy dating "in," which is a great option for when you have a little baby, or a sick child, or can't quite afford a night out on a particular weekend. I'll let my friends speak out on that in this chapter's Dish. But there is something enlivening about leaving the building for a time even if it's just two or three hours. And I do practice what I'm preachin' here. Doyle and I are movie buffs, so we try to get out and see a flick every three or four weeks. We talk in the car on the way there, we experience the movie together, and then we go for dessert afterward and hang out. Yes, we may be in a rut, but it works for us. We love to spend that time together engaging in a mutually enjoyable pastime. We always come back perkier and more in tune with each other.

Because of my job as a freelance entertainment writer for the local newspaper, Doyle and I also see quite a few concerts together. Rock, pop, country, R&B, classical—you name the genre, we've seen it. Doyle especially enjoys hearing a live band, and those concert nights have been wonderful bonding times. (Well, he didn't enjoy being dragged to Michael Bolton so much, or Jessica Simpson, either, come to think of it!)

To get out of the dinner-and-a-movie habit, try having your own one-on-one book club (which will get you talking about things other than this week's teething updates) or pool tournament for two. Even if you don't know a cue ball from an eightball, there's something seductive about prowling around a pool table. Go in-line skating, fish, or take ballroom dancing or salsa lessons. Visit art galleries, go to a monster truck rally. Hike, bike, or dogsled (if you really want to give "mush mush" a new meaning). Whatever you do, get out of the house and revel in the company of the one who used to make you weak in the knees.

✿ "TONIGHT, TONIGHT, WON'T BE JUST ANY NIGHT"

For many people, a week away from home is impossible, but most of us could chisel out a weekend or even one night away per year. Doyle and I usually go away for our anniversary in November (see "Cocoa Cottage"). For us, this annual getaway celebrates our union and gives us a chance to take inventory, increase our closeness, and just hang out together, our reverie unbroken by the nonstop chatter of little boys.

Even a solitary weekend or night away can be a true tonic for parents who want to be lovers again. Journalist Elizabeth Fishel describes the good medicine that her annual night away with her husband provides. As their babies became boys, the honeymoon stage of being new parents faded, and Fishel and her husband were ready to resuscitate their old habit of going away together. "We yearned to be the soul mates we once were," she wrote, amigos who shared recreational pursuits, lingered over leisurely dinners out, and made each other laugh like no one else did. But had their hyperfocus on their sons buried those connections so deeply that the Fishels would need much more than a night away? After all, with no extended family nearby, she found it complicated enough to eke out one night away. She comments, "The marching orders we left behind for our baby-sitters rivaled the plan for the invasion of Normandy."

Fishel and her husband went in spite of the long list of detailed instructions, and they were rewarded with a wonderful time of hiking, soaking in the hot tub, eating by candlelight, sleeping late, and focusing on no one but themselves. Since that wondrous night, the couple have made their rendezvous an annual event. "Our night away has become an oasis in the helter-skelter of child-raising," she said. "We slowly turn back into the people we were before we got derailed by diaper changes and midnight feedings, school meetings and soccer games."[5]

One dad had been in a fog about why his sex life had taken such a hit since the birth of his first child. But when he and his wife finally got away for a couple of days, he was finally able to put his finger on the problem: "After the kids were old enough for us to leave them with Grandma for a weekend, we escaped to a romantic getaway at the coast, and it was like someone had poured gasoline on smoldering coals. Suddenly the fire returned and we were like, 'Oh...so that's what was missing.'"[6]

In the enchanting, mysterious luster of a yearly overnight or weekend away, you can find that missing piece of the puzzle. You can rediscover the people you were and the relationship you had before the munchkins arrived. You can truly create your own special marriage-renewing ritual. Lisa B. and her husband, parents of three and under the thumb of a tight budget, received an overnight getaway as a gift: "It was like we were two different people!" she told me. "Affectionate! Happy! Attentive! Sexy! It was so reassuring to *remember* what we could be together and what will come back around in time."

If the thought of leaving your offspring for a night or two still makes you feel disloyal, keep in mind that you will talk about them—and probably a lot. Like Elizabeth Fishel, you'll relish their achievements and personalities and mull over their issues—with the extravagance of not having them two feet away, needing your attention at any moment. Reinvigorated, you'll return to your children closer partners and more effective parents.

My friend Joy works full time as a biology professor, and she and her family live away from both sets of grandparents. Yet four times a year, Joy and Chad get away together for at least one night, leaving four-year-old Meikea with friends. "Our getaways are vital for us," she says. "When we are alone, it allows us to invest in each other and play together. So much of our lives revolves around making decisions as parents and homeowners and so on. We need to play sometimes! The other weekend we cross-country skied, went out to eat, talked and talked, and of course we enjoyed each other physically. Some of my friends have made comments like, 'Is it wise to leave your child?' or 'I could never leave my child.' I always say,

'We have to leave her once in a while. It's not optional. She will be with us for fourteen more years, but we will be together forever.'"

The Sisterhood of the Traveling Moms

Jennifer was a new mom who once loved to travel. Her scrapbooks were filled with photos of blue skies, mountain vistas, and aqua paradises. Even after the birth of her baby, Jennifer and her husband went on a cruise to the Caribbean, toting three-month-old Matthew along. Now ten months old, Matthew's not quite as portable as he was seven months ago. As Jennifer sat cropping photos of a trip to Alaska she took a few years ago, she talked enthusiastically about various destinations she would love to hit.

"Would you guys go by yourselves?" I asked, already knowing the answer.

"No," she said quietly. "I couldn't leave him."

"Of course not," I replied. "He's still a baby. That's totally natural. But someday probably you will be able to leave him with someone you trust."

I hoped for Jennifer's sake that statement was true. If you want to jump-start a sluggish marriage, there's nothing quite like a night away, a weekend at a B&B, or maybe even a week-long trip experiencing a new place and building memories.

Maybe my wish for Jennifer was so fervent because I, too, adore travel. For me, the prospect of journeying to a different locale—hopefully a different country—fills me with a sense of excitement and verve that nothing else touches. Travel, Doyle and I have finally concluded, is to me what the outdoors and hunting and fishing are to him. It feeds my soul and gratifies my spirit like nothing else.

When I was just a little bit pregnant with Jonah, I went to Europe to visit some friends. This little voyage, though peppered with bouts of morning sickness and pregnancy-induced fatigue, scratched the itch for quite some time. After bringing home my blue-eyed baby boy, I was so enthralled with him, so utterly committed to his well-being, that I couldn't imagine leaving him. Like many new moms, I was attached body and soul to my baby, and he was about a year old before Doyle and I even ventured away overnight.

But by the time Jonah was two, I was ready to travel again. After months of poring over travel brochures and the Internet, Doyle and I decided to visit Costa Rica for eight days. Jonah would stay with his doting grandparents, safe and sound and doing very well for himself indeed while we were gallivanting in Central America. I'll never forget, though, the almost tearing sensation that I experienced when I hugged Jonah good-bye on my in-laws' front porch. I tried to be cheery, but anyone could tell I was fighting tears. (Doyle was absolutely fine. I think this wrenching apart is mostly a mom phenomenon).

Did I miss my chubby-cheeked toddler? Yes, terribly at times.

I had his photo handy almost all the time during the trip. I was ready to whip it out and foist it upon Costa Rican cabdrivers, river-raft guides, and honeymooning couples by the pool.

But as the trip evolved, with its horseback rides in the rain-forest, river-rafting thrills and spills, soaks in thermal pools at the base of a volcano, dinners à deux with our toes digging in the sand of a beachfront restaurant…sigh…a part of me that I had buried in the good work of mothering resurfaced. It felt amazing.

What our trip to Costa Rica did for us as a couple—and there-fore as a family—was truly wondrous. Doyle and I were together on an adventure, building memories and having a ball. The expe-rience of being lifted out of our ordinary world and exposed to new phenomena at every turn revitalized us as a twosome. As a team, we tasted new foods, made new friends, and tried new experiences. And, yes, as we knit our hearts together again, we fell in love again. It sounds corny, but it's true. (And, naturally, on our own in such a sensual locale, we had the inkling and energy to hit the sack—among other places—like a couple of honeymooners. We even have the kid to prove it: Ezra!)

When we emerged from that airplane back on U.S. soil, we were as much soul mates as we ever were, simpatico, tuned-in, and ready to face the new phase of family life together. Our little jaunt actually inspired friends of ours to leave their daughter with grand-parents while they soaked up the sun at a Mexican spa. Some people would definitely think such an expedition selfish or indulgent, but truly this escapade probably saved their marriage and preserved their family.

George and Emily, whom we met earlier, were pregnant again and decided to go to Jamaica for four days to recharge their couplehood before Baby Number Two's arrival. Emily raved about the benefits of their trip, including replenishing their energy and strengthening their bond to better face a family crisis that met them upon their return to Michigan. (No, the crisis had nothing to do with their toddler, Vera. George's mom had been in a car accident, which, to make a long story short, led to George's donating a kidney to her.)

Sometimes the realities of life with children make it difficult, if not impossible, to steal away for a partners' vacation. Oftentimes Grandma is not simply over the hill and through the woods, but a plane ride away. As much as I value our time alone together, I doubt we would have gone anywhere, let alone to another country, had Doyle's parents not been willing and able to care for our child. Sick kids, limited time off from work, and financial restraints also conspire to deter the mom-and-pop holiday. But if you do have the option of leaving your kiddies with loving caregivers, by all means consider a second honeymoon, even if it's camping for a week at a nearby KOA. You won't believe the difference it can make in your love life!

✿ THE DISH: "NO ONE HAS AN EXCUSE!"

On this subject of getting out, my Dish friends are divided. Some of them rave about regular getaways with the father of their children; others are frustrated by obstacles that keep them from getting out the door. All, however, agree on the importance of making time to be alone with hubby, whether at home or away.

Perhaps the biggest factor that gets in the way of old-fashioned dating is the cost of baby-sitting. For Amy Q., a mother of five kids, paying a baby-sitter at least $2.50 a child per hour adds up to $12.50 per hour. Pretty prohibitive. Lisa B. knows what that's like. She and her husband don't have family nearby. "We were better about a date night twice a month before Baby Number Three," Lisa says. "We'd still be having our dates, but the third child has really stretched our budget to the limit—and now baby-sitters are even more expensive. It's really hard to justify, even when we know it's cheaper than marriage counseling!" Can't cough up the cash for a baby-sitter? Many young couples have success swapping an evening of baby-sitting with some friends or even with their own siblings who also have kids. The point is, find a way to leave your children and be together.

Amy Q. and her mate, Steve, solve their problem by linking up under their own roof: "Steve and I try to date 'in' every other week. We feed the kids early, get them to bed, then order Chinese, and sit and talk. *No movies!* We light the candles and reminisce about our romantic dating days," she said. "We like to play the 'favorites' game: 'What is your favorite _____?' With having to remember to change, feed, and clothe kids all day long, it's easy for me to forget what my hubby likes. By the way, this can lead to some interesting foreplay or even positions!" Well, well, well. Sounds like Amy is onto something there…

Fortunately for the Q's, Grandma does live in town, so they also leave the building on occasion. "We do try to go out at least once or twice a month," she says. "We set a day and *stick to it!* Once a year we try to sneak away for a long weekend, and last year we even got away for a week! If we can do it with five kids under eight, no one has an excuse! Our pastor's 'strong suggestion' to date every week and get away with your mate for a weekend each year have been much appreciated."

When asked about how often she and her husband cop alone time, Erika played the twins card—not that I blame her! "We are actually pretty bad about regular getaways," she admitted. "Two reasons: (1) We tended to be homebodies before the babies came, and (2) our babies have really only settled into any sort of reliable nighttime routine in the past couple of months—now that they're almost one year old!" Like Amy, Erika also found that "in" dating scratched the itch, especially when her twins were young babies. "We like to cook together, and this is a real pleasant bonding time for us, something we've carried over from our prebaby days," she says. "Usually we put the kids to bed first, or sometimes we put them in their baby backpacks and bop around the kitchen as a happy foursome. Then, by the time we eat, the kids are definitely in bed, and we can just chill. Granted, this means that we often eat after seven thirty, but it's worth the relaxing, enjoyable time together."

Mary and her main man shoot for once-a-week dates, which usually means they end up toasting each other with java at their local Starbucks. "We're definitely getting old," Mary laughs. But, hey, getting out once a week is fantastic. Most couples don't achieve nearly that much in the way of outings.

Dan and Ann try to date once a month. "Some months we do better than others," says Ann. "It just takes planning and follow-through. My favorite thing to do is go out to dinner. I like eating out, and the time at the restaurant gives us time to talk. Going to movies is fun too, but we can rarely agree on what to see, and you can't talk during a movie."

A great date can happen as close as your own neighborhood, says Lisa H. "We do have date nights, but simple things—for example, today we took a long walk together in a park—seem the most romantic at this point," she admits. "Getaways are pretty unrealistic for us with no family support nearby."

Those who do have the freedom to leave for a night or two, however, rave about the benefits: "Ray and I went to the Michael W. Smith concert and stayed overnight at the Amway Grand Hotel, this fancy hotel in downtown Grand Rapids," Ann B. enthused. "It was such a departure from our normal, crazy world with four kids—it was heavenly. We even ordered room service—fixings for banana splits—and made them ourselves in our room. And, yes, Ray definitely got lucky that night—and so did I!"

In or out, the goal is to get away from your wipe-a-nose workaday surroundings and see one another in a new light.

✿ DESPERATELY SEEKING MRS. DOUBTFIRE

Sometimes even when you can afford a baby-sitter, finding one is a problem. Just ask Twila: "One of the main reasons that we did not go out on dates for a while (years!) after our son was born was the lack of baby-sitters," Twila says. "We went to a large church but didn't know many people. Our parents lived several hours away. Our friends lived on the opposite end of town."

And, believe it or not, not all grandmas are big on baby-sitting. One of my girlfriends confessed that she was shocked and devastated when her mom announced she would not be baby-sitting the grandchildren—any of them! "You mean she didn't want to do day care forty hours a week?" I asked. "Nope," said Kris. "She doesn't want to baby-sit for even one night. It's totally weird." I'll say! Thankfully, that story isn't the norm. Usually grandparents are dying to spend time with their grandbabies.

I know some people who never leave their children with anyone but Grandma or Aunt Cindy. I'm not sure what to say about that because Doyle and I have had marvelous success finding and keeping trustworthy sitters. We even developed close relationships with our main girls. Jonah was a ring bearer for his first baby-sitter, Karina, when she got married. I can understand parents' reluctance to leave their beloved baby with someone they don't know, but if the child is into the toddler years, that's really no excuse. Some people worry that they might accidentally hire a psycho teen or some kind of neglectful airhead who will allow their baby to play with knives. This won't happen if you find a sitter with great references (as in, your friend has used her and says she's the bomb), she is part of a community you trust (like church or your college alma mater), and you have a good feeling about her. If you must, call the sitter six times while you're having dinner, but do step out for dates on a regular basis.

I hope our success stories encourage you. We found Karina through a friend from church who commended both the girl and her family. They had come from Peru years before so Dad could start up a ministry to Spanish-speaking families in Grand Rapids. We met with Karina once before she baby-sat alone, and instantly we felt a kinship with her. She was obviously a sensible, mature girl who would take good care of our baby. Unfortunately, Karina was already sixteen when we found her, so her baby-sitting days were starting to wane. But her younger sister, Grace, then fourteen, became our baby-sitter for the next three years. Grace asked us one summer Saturday if she could practice her Backyard Bible Club flannel-board lesson on Jonah. Um, sure!

When Grace retired from baby-sitting, we found Helen, again through a church friend. I knew Helen's mom through a Bible study I went to. Helen, we think, may be more trustworthy than we are! When we come home from our night out, we usually find her watching the History Channel or reading a book. Our back-up girl is Jordana, who, adopted from Ethiopia, somberly told me that her dream is to open an orphanage in Africa. It's like having a young Mother Teresa watch our kids!

All this to say, there are good and even great baby-sitters out there, and they aren't that hard to find.

TREVOR AND DEB GET OUT

In the end, Deb decided to go out for dinner with Trevor. On the day of their anniversary, he kissed her in the morning before he went to work, saying, "Happy anniversary, boo. I can't wait until tonight." She smiled at his use of *boo,* his nickname for her from when they were dating. She was still apprehensive about leaving Avery at night—her sleeping schedule could be so erratic—but her nervousness was mingled with anticipation. Still, what to wear? None of her prebaby clothes fit, and all her new clothes were too casual. Deb made a quick run to her favorite clothing store with Avery. It wasn't easy to shop with a toddler running around, but Deb managed to find something kind of pretty and flattering that would work for the dinner.

Trevor had made reservations at Cygnus, a beautiful restaurant at the top of a skyscraper in their city. On the way, Debra was quiet, even a little tearful over leaving Avery. She was grateful, though, that Trevor had been patient with this. In the car he covered her hand with his, a gesture that seemed comforting and sweet.

By the time they were seated at the restaurant, Debra was starting to feel more at ease. It was fun to peruse the menu, which she noticed had no chicken nuggets or hot dogs on it. With Avery not there, Deb also had time to look around and take in her posh surroundings. "It feels weird, not having to cut anyone's meat," Debra said, smiling ruefully at Trevor.

"You can cut mine if it makes you feel better," he said, smiling back.

They laughed a little at this and continued to look over their menus. After the waiter took their orders, Trevor whipped out his cell phone to call home and find out how Avery was doing. Deb realized she hadn't even thought about calling until that moment. Avery was fine, Grandma reported. She was having her bath next and then it was on to bed.

"She's in good hands, you know," Trevor said to Deb when he finished talking to his mom.

"I know," she responded.

For the next hour or so, Trevor and Deb talked about his work, the possibility of them moving in the next year or so, problems at their church, his brother's upcoming wedding, the new Brad Pitt movie, and, of course, Avery. But Trevor was surprised that their daughter wasn't the main topic of conversation. He adored his chubby little tot, but there was something refreshing about chatting with Deb about other stuff. It was over dessert, crème brûlée for him and chocolate flan for her, that he ventured a little flirting.

"You look good," he said, wiggling his eyebrows at his wife.

"I do?" she said, pleased. Deb couldn't remember the last time Trevor had complimented her appearance.

"Yeah."

Deb grinned at Trevor. "You look good yourself, for someone's dad," she said.

"Hey, just because I'm someone's dad doesn't mean I can't be a hottie." They laughed at her teenage sister's favorite expression.

After dessert, they drove toward home. Instead of taking their exit, though, Trevor steered the car in another direction.

"Where are we going?" Deb asked.

"Oh, you'll see, you'll see." Trevor winked at her.

Within minutes, they pulled into the parking lot of a riverside recreation area they sometimes took Avery to. When they were first married, Trevor and Deb used to jog there all the time.

"What are we doing here?" she asked, curious and a bit tense. It was getting late. Had Avery gone down okay? If Trevor noticed the edge in Deb's voice, he didn't comment. Instead, he switched the car off and turned in his seat to face her.

"This is the point where I should give you a fantastic anniversary present," he said, "but I messed up and didn't actually get you anything."

"I didn't get you anything either," Deb said, wondering where this was going.

"That's okay. Anniversaries are for women anyway," he said, smiling. "But I wanted to tell you something, before we got home, in case Avery woke up or something." Trevor cleared his throat and looked a bit sheepish. "I guess I just wanted to say that you're an amazing mom. You do so much for our daughter. I love you. Happy anniversary, Deb."

Debra melted. Trevor never talked to her like that anymore. She didn't even care about the present. Last year he had gotten her a new breast pump, so she hadn't exactly been expecting diamonds.

They drove home in silence, both of them content and at ease with each other for the first time in ages. Avery was fast asleep when they arrived. Bedtime had gone fairly smoothly, although Deb's mom said Avery had cried for about twenty minutes. Deb felt a twinge of guilt. If she had been there, Avery wouldn't have cried. Well, maybe she would have, but at least her mommy could have comforted her.

Deb peeked in on her daughter and then went to get ready for bed. For the first time since Avery was born, Deb considered wearing something different than her usual oversized 5K-run T-shirt from college. Usually, though, Trevor stayed up late and watched television on weekend nights. It might be pointless to get all gussied up if he wasn't even going to show. Then she heard his footsteps in the hall.

"Hey, boo," he said, eyes twinkling.

"Hey," she said, twinkling back. The whole matter of sleep-wear had just become moot.

Mojo Makeover: Get Out, Get Out, Wherever You Are

Establish a Date Night

Agree on a date night and stick to it! If something comes up, like one of your kids gets the flu, be sure to reschedule right away.

Leave Annually

Once a year—at least—invest in your family's primary relationship and go away for a night or two. As you just read, there's nothing like it for rejuvenating your marriage and jump-starting your sex life again!

Leave for Longer

Consider taking a longer trip together. I'm not saying you should book a cruise when the baby is six months old, but when your kids are at a good age—in most cases eighteen months and older—a week with Grandma and Grandpa would likely be a fun thing for everyone. Mom, you'll miss the kids, and you'll probably want to call the trip off six times before you even leave, but keep in mind the incredible tonic a Mom-and-Pop adventure could be for you two. Remember: *Anything that's good for your marriage is good for your kids!*

❀ TALES FROM THE LOVE SHACK: COCOA COTTAGE

We were approaching our twelfth anniversary, my good husband and I. Now, November 9 falls smack-dab in the middle of hunting season. Well, it falls right before gun season and right at the end of bow season, which, in my husband's book, makes it perhaps the worst time for an anniversary to fall.

Like every hunting season that had come and gone since we exchanged rings that snowy, glorious day in arctic Winnipeg, the ebb and flow of our marriage was at a low tide. The daughter of a city bookseller, I had never become accustomed to either the gleam in Doyle's eye that had nothing to do with me or the glazed-over look he sported between late August and late November.

That year, for whatever reason, seemed more fractious and loveless than the others. Doyle felt that he had to beg, borrow, and steal hours to indulge in the hobby that he loved, and I felt that only if I grew antlers would my husband consider me appealing once more. Maybe. We tensely negotiated good times for Doyle to go hunting, times that wouldn't infringe too terribly on my work-on-Saturdays routine. Of course, because Doyle has a job, Saturdays are prime hunting days. Often we found ourselves at an impasse, and more than once we fought quite bitterly.

Some women deal with golf, hockey, softball, and so on. Hunting was my personal marital Waterloo. Feeling more like opponents than friends—never mind lovers—Doyle and I both sensed we needed to find our way back to each other.

One day he surprised me with an e-mail, saying he had checked out the Web site for this great bed-and-breakfast I had read about in the newspaper's travel section. "Should I book us for the eighth and ninth?" he wondered.

"Book us!" was the ebullient response I shot off into cyberspace. The knowledge that my sometimes faraway husband would take the initiative to go away during hunting season softened my cranky hunter's-widow self. So he booked us for two nights at Cocoa Cottage. Even the name summoned images of crackling fires, cozy places to cuddle, and chocolaty sensuality.

Hunting season marched on, but like the pot of gold at the end of the rainbow, Cocoa Cottage waited in the distance. Even on days when, truth be told, we couldn't stand each other, we still had this beacon of light to help get us through.

The day dawned, and we drove the boys out to their grand-parents' house in Muskegon, a mere fifteen-minute drive away from the adorable town of Whitehall and our romantic destination. Cocoa Cottage was all that and a bag of Hershey's Kisses. Meticulously restored to its Arts and Crafts roots, the cozy B&B exuded warmth and welcome.

Our room was on the small side, which only made it more conducive to bumping into each other. I oohed and aahed over the small details that gave the room its charm. Mirrors from 1914, a bed piled high with luxuriously soft linens, and handmade chocolates in exquisite little period dishes all added up to a feeling of indulgence.

Larry and Lisa, the innkeepers, held a first-night reception for us and the other two couples staying with them that weekend. We dined on chocolate-dipped strawberries, heavenly flourless cake, and the most amazing artichoke dip I had ever eaten. We laughed at the antics of the two other couples, both old enough to be our parents and seasoned in the craft of marriage keeping. We bowled for the first time in ten years at an alley freeze-dried in the fifties, throwing strikes and gutter balls both to the sonic bubbles of the Platters and the Temptations. We found ourselves loosening up, the knots of resentment and the tightness of the daily grind unraveling with each hour.

But we didn't make love. Not the first night, anyway. We were so tired that by mutual agreement we decided to postpone any nooky for the following night. Even so, in the otherworldliness of the inn and the sheer joy of having fun together, we began to connect the dots again. Cuddling on the couch, we watched the film *Chocolat* (what else?). Then, following the decadent aroma of chocolate that had wafted into the living room, we teamed up to sneak to the kitchen.

Innkeeper's Recipe for Marriage

Our innkeepers at Cocoa Cottage, Larry and Lisa Tallarico, concoct a line of divine hot-fudge sauces bottled under their own "Mama Tallarico's" brand. The last morning we were with them, we were presented with a jar of sauce, custom-labeled with our names and anniversary date. Nifty, eh? On the back of the jar was the following prescribed list of ingredients and instructions for a union as luscious as chocolate:

"Marriage is a blending of the sweetness of two unique individuals. In harmony they yoke to form the exquisite mixture that no two others can achieve.

"Ingredients: True love, patience, trust, respect, honesty, compassion, humor, and forgiveness.

"Mama suggests you heat it up, pour on the good times, celebrate your differences, fold in your accomplishments, and savor your desserts. Love each other for who you are and maintain respect at all times."

That night we fell asleep content and connected for the first time in weeks. The next day things got a little flirtier, and it was obvious that this night would be a little different from the previous one! We rediscovered antiquing, an old pastime gone by the wayside since we'd had kids. I rummaged through a bunch of dusty old books, and Doyle checked out a vintage forge he thought his dad the blacksmith might want. Driving through country roads lined with coppery trees, we could have been a million miles away from our kids rather than just twenty. Lunch at a nearby ranch, with a spectacular view of the golf course and fall foliage below our window, only underscored our intensifying feeling of stepping out of reality and into a galaxy where couplehood trumped parenthood. Of course I missed the little munchkins, and so did their dad, but we knew that reupholstering the rather threadbare love seat of our union would do them as much or more good as it was doing us.

The other Cocoa Cottage guests—a wild and crazy bunch if there ever was one—teased us incessantly about doing "research" for the very book you hold in your hands. Playing cards with them until late into the night, we were the target of many little asides and double entendres. The hassling was all in good fun, and we gave as good as we got. Odd as it may sound, it was kind of comforting to know that mature folks like our new friends were still so red-blooded. "Hope for the future," Doyle said, grinning.

Plied with sumptuous food, delectable chocolate, and lots and lots of laughter—which boosts oxygen and blood flow, as a matter of fact—we finally ambled upstairs to the privacy of our cozy boudoir. And yes, somewhere between the chocolate zucchini bread of that day's breakfast and the chocolate crumb cake of the following morning, we became lovers again.

No new moves were trotted out for the occasion, nor any gimmicky outfits—although when I was packing, the thought of getting a camo negligee had crossed my mind. It was just plain old lovemaking, ramped up a few notches by a change of scenery, focused time nurturing each other, and the joy of regeneration. Oh, and the high dosage of the primeval aphrodisiac, le cocoa bean, didn't hurt either.

We returned to our children, renewed, refreshed, and—let's face it—hot for each other. The passion and camaraderie of the weekend lingered for weeks, smoothing over the last potentially bumpy stretch of hunting season.

Recently I ran into one of the funny ladies from the weekend in the restroom of a theater. After some excited chatter about what we had been up to, Kay, a fifty-something babe with a great sense of humor, leaned in and said, with a twinkle in her eyes, "Lorilee, how's that 'research' coming along?"

"Couldn't be better, Kay," I replied, twinkling right back at her. "Thanks for asking."

Sparkplugs: A Sprinkle a Day
Keeps the Sex Therapist Away

I have a friend whose mother cracked a rib falling in the shower.
"Apparently my parents were getting a little bit frisky," she ex-
plained. I gaped at her, slack jawed with awe and grateful I didn't
have to own a similar visual of my own parents! In my opinion,
shower sex can be dangerous—and not just for women my
mother's age. Jacuzzi sex is much easier and much less threatening
to life and limb. Still, I hear about people doing it in the shower all
the time. Here are two reports from my Dish files:

- "It may seem like a small thing, but showering together
  has made a world of difference in the way we stay connected. It's something we have to do anyway, so we do it
  together. We actually had a his-and-hers shower installed
  so one of us wouldn't be cold while the other one is hot
  and comfortable. Once we're both hot and soapy, that's
  when things start getting interesting! Seriously, though,
  most nights we just talk about whatever is going on in
  our lives. Kids, money, jobs, church, in-laws, who will
  win *Survivor.* In the shower we slow down, relax, and
  reconnect in a meaningful way. Of course, in smoothing
  any tension between us, it helps that we are both naked.
  It's hard to be mad at a naked person! And the sensuality
  of being hot and soapy gives new meaning to the phrase

getting yourself in a lather! Yes, since we started this shower-
for-two thing, our sex life has improved quite drastically."
—Krista

- "Three words: *hit the showers!* Since Gabby isn't such a
  great sleeper, Bart and I are usually bone tired. Sex can be
  at the bottom of our priorities. The best solution we've
  found is shower time. About three times a week, we lock
  the bathroom door and lather up. Nine times out of ten,
  something good will come of it, either shower sex or just a
  really good uninterrupted conversation. The bottom line is
  that we stay intimate even when it's been a really crazy day
  with the kids or at work or whatever. Once in a while we
  even continue the romance in our bed, which of course is
  way easier!" —Jannie

FOUR

Yeah Girl, You Just Pushed a Baby Through There!

Beating the Libido Busters, Part 1:
Sex After Six Weeks

I n the previous chapter, our parental units Trevor and Debra did in fact reclaim some of their lost passion. Of course, as we all know, the road to a great sex life is pitted with potholes, and this mom and dad have plenty of those to traverse before completely getting their groove back.

Nine months after Trevor and Debra's fifth anniversary, Micah was born, a chubby little boy with an adorable smile and a serious case of colic. Neither of Micah's parents got much sleep in the months following his birth, and both were obviously a little ragged around the edges.

But one morning Trevor and Debra woke up and realized they had slept through the night. Turns out, Micah was done with screaming for hours and hours, thank goodness! Gradually, things returned to normal in the Arbuckle household as Avery adjusted to her new baby brother and their parents adjusted to having two kids.

Unfortunately, *normal* for Trevor and Deb meant that their sex life was still lacking. This was especially disappointing because things had improved in that area after the night of their fifth anniversary. Debra had become much more willing to leave Avery, and the two felt more connected as a result of their dates. This connection carried over into the bedroom, and both felt they had recaptured a small measure of passion that had been lost when Avery was born.

Of course, Debra's pregnancy brought its own challenges, including twice the weight gain she'd had with Avery. Trevor didn't care about the extra weight gain. He thought Debra was beautiful, if a little cranky, when she was pregnant. He tried to roll with the hormonal ups and downs, and for the most part he succeeded. Basically, Trevor was just delighted that Deb had snapped out of the baby-induced fog she had been in for the eighteen months prior. They could hang out together and go to movies and out for dinner, and she didn't obsess about Avery nearly as much.

After Micah's birth, though, Trevor felt as though their marriage was once again shoved to the back burner. As it turned out, the reasons Debra drifted away from him this time were different. With Avery, Debra was glued to the baby—physically of course, but mentally, too, in a way that blocked out everything and everyone, including Trevor. In Micah's case, though she dearly loved her son, his screaming fits made her more than willing to hand him over to one of the grandparents for a few hours. She needed time to herself or she would crack up, she thought.

Between soothing Micah at night and caring for Avery during the day, Debra was more tired than she thought possible. Trevor understood that—he was often up at night too. Who could sleep through all that screaming? But even when Micah calmed down—and when he did, he was a surprisingly happy, contented baby—Deb still didn't seem all that interested in Trevor as a companion, a husband, or a lover for that matter. She treated him, he felt, as a roommate or the guy who paid the bills. Any romantic advances on his part were ignored or outright rejected, and Debra's rejection stung.

Ah, yes. There's nothing like a couple of new parents (or new-again parents) seamlessly resuming their nights of wild passion the very moment Dr. Zhivago—or whoever—gives the green light. Right.

More likely the husband and the husband alone is raring to go, practically wasting away after a lacuna of six weeks, bare minimum. True, he's been almost as overwhelmed as his wife by the demands of a newborn, sleep deprivation, and the three-week visit from his lovely mother-in-law. But the guy is beyond ready to hit the sheets once more. If only he had a willing partner.

Mom, on the other hand, would rather fall out of an airplane than get frisky. Why does the appearance of a ten-pound bundle of joy so thoroughly smash one's sex life to smithereens? (*Why, why, why?* the husband asks.)

I'm here to tell you—and not just because I'm a woman and would like to defend my sisters out there: new moms have so many things going on in their bodies and minds that conspire against sexuality it's a wonder anyone ever gets it on again after delivering a baby.

Here are some likely culprits:

1. YOU'RE WAY, WAY TOO TIRED

Uh-huh. You would doze off right now if you could. During Baby's first year, a new parent loses between 400 and 750 hours of sleep. To add insult to injury, the quality of sleep is actually poorer because Baby gets you up every couple of hours. That means that both the deep, physically restorative sleep and the psychologically beneficial dream stages are cut short. You could be irritable, depressed, anxious, and antisocial. No wonder you find sex an almost laughably impractical venture. Sleep is just plain key to a sane life. No shocker, then, that the whopping majority of new mamas choose snooze over wild, raging *amoré*.

Not to discourage you, but the problem of fatigue isn't something that will go away anytime soon. It's a theme that comes up time and time again in discussions about sex and motherhood. Veteran moms, too, complain of feeling drained of energy and confess to shoving passion once more to the back burner in favor of some much-needed slumber. Being too weary for sex was far and away the biggest obstacle to lovemaking that my gang of Dish moms reported. It's no surprise that Amy Q., turbo-mama of five kids under the age of eight, is often dead on her feet at the end of the day. "I need more *energy!*" she says. "This is so hard for me to come to terms with because there are times I want to be in the mood and just can't get my head off the pillow to give Steve a kiss!"

We've all been there! Sleep is the easy choice, and it's hard to summon up any enthusiasm for a roll in the hay when what you truly want and need is eight solid hours of REM. Plus, sleep is more important to baseline functioning, isn't it? You're not going to drive off the side of the road and hit a phone pole if you haven't had enough sex, but you just might if you don't sleep enough. Even though it seems as if you must make a choice between the two, that doesn't have to be the case.

Mojo Makeover: A decent night's sleep, or even a short nap on a Saturday afternoon, can do wonders for your energy level—and your interest in sex. Ask a friend to watch your kids or hire a sitter to help you accomplish this. It's worth the money!

Also, try making love earlier rather than later. I'm not a morning person by any stretch of the imagination. But libido is highest in the morning, and I've been very pleasantly surprised with first-thing nooky after some solid shuteye and before the kids arise. My pal Emily suggests this pretty good solution: "We've found that if we leave sex until after Vera's in bed and it's late, we are just too pooped. To keep up on a healthy 'schedule,' afternoon delights (during her naptime) are great as well as very early bedtimes together."

❀ 2. It Hurts

Let's say Mom's labor was of average intensity (and by that I mean no third-degree tearing or other hideous delivery events). She's most likely still sore down yonder even months after delivering.

Few expect sex to be uncomfortable for much longer than the first couple of months after birth. And yet it often is, sometimes for much, much longer. After so much disuse, one's vagina is as dry as dust, adding to the pain. Of course, that's why K-Y jelly was invented.

Mojo Makeover: Grab a tube and go slooooow. Experiment with different positions. Your man is unlikely to care which position as long as it is something. Since the traditional missionary position tends to put pressure right on the area that's likely to be most sore—your perineum—you might prefer to make love lying side by side or with you on top.

3. IT FEELS ODD

If you gave birth vaginally, your vagina may feel a little slack for a while. One benefit of C-sections, if I do say so, is that this particular problem is never an issue. (Writer Vicki Iovine, of the *Girlfriends' Guides* fame, brags that C-section moms retain "the vaginal tone of a teenager," which might be of some comfort to all of you who wished desperately for a natural birth and had to go the C-section route.)

Mojo Makeover: If you feel as if your tone ain't what it used to be, do your Kegel exercises faithfully, and you'll regain much of your vaginal muscle. What are Kegels? A wonderful humanitarian named Dr. Arnold Kegel—a man!—came up with this little exercise for his female patients who were encountering incontinence and other problems after childbirth. First, the next time you pay a visit to the W.C., identify the pertinent muscle by stopping the flow of your urine midstream. Got it? Yeah, it's that muscle. To do Kegels, flex that muscle and count to ten as you hold it tight. Release for a few seconds, then flex and hold again. Repeat this ten times as often as you think about it during the day. The beauty of

Kegels is that you can do them anywhere, anytime, and no one will ever know! The more you work it, girl, the tighter your muscle will be. And the tighter it is, the more fireworks will occur during climax. This tip is for all women, but new moms will benefit the most because of their newly loosened muscles.

4. YOUR ESTROGEN IS AWOL

This is a huge factor in the sex-after-baby slump: Postpartum women are estrogen deprived because the placenta is no longer there. During pregnancy your placenta instead of your ovaries produces estrogen. And no estrogen equals not much desire. Picture your car's gas tank running on a fume and a prayer. That's what's going on with your "estrogen tank." Can you imagine your husband suddenly and severely testosterone deprived? Neither can he, which is part of the problem. Testosterone makes him hot for you, just as estrogen makes you warm for his form. Well, it used to anyway...

Mojo Makeover: Again, talk it over with your guy. Let him in on the news flash that your natural lust-boosters are AWOL for the time being anyway. Until your ovaries kick in—which can take a month or so if you're not breast-feeding and from six months to a year if you are—you'll be low on estrogen and therefore low on desire. Hopefully just sharing this information with your husband will give him a big "aha" moment, and he'll be more patient. The man will probably be grateful to know your lack of lust is not personal—he's still as studly as ever—but rather a real biological side effect of giving birth.

5. BREAST-FEEDING: GOOD FOR BABY, BAD FOR SEX LIFE

Breast-feeding is fantastic for your baby, both physically and emotionally. But months and months of exclusive nursing can do a huge number on your sex drive. Dr. Pierre Assalian, the chief psychiatrist at Montreal General's Department of Psychiatry, warns that breast-feeding women produce prolactin, a hormone that can "kill" libido.[1] That's right, women. He used the word "kill." My friend Janelle was actually relieved to hear this medical fact because, eight weeks after having Baby Number Three, Serena, she felt as if she had just somehow turned into an asexual turnip. "Right now I don't care if it's a year before we start doing it again," she said. "But I'm glad it's not just me."

So we have this big issue of prolactin, which supports the production of breast milk and also serves as a major lust buster. By the way, prolactin also thwarts the production of your body's natural lubricants, so between it and your lack of estrogen, things down under will be positively desertlike. In addition to these hormonal components, there's the very compelling "my boobs belong to Baby" factor. Breast-feeding is incredibly physical, and when you're doing it six times a day, having your breasts touched one more time is one time too many for many moms. "My body was in constant use by the baby," Tracy says. "So when my husband came on to me, it felt like one more person needing something from me. I was touched out by the end of the day."

Some guys report being unsettled by the new deli-bar aspect of their wife's body. It may be chic to have a milk bath at the spa, but there is something disconcerting about being mid-act and having a spray of dairylike product squirt from your wife's breasts. Can we be quite frank? If your husband is doing any kind of kissing or licking, he may get a whole lot more than he bargained for. I've heard of guys getting an eyeful or noseful of milk, which slows things down, to say the least. You could laugh at the obvious absurdity of it and then move on, or you could become mortified by the strangeness of your lover blowing his nose after inhaling a spritz of breast milk. Either way, the momentum is broken. Jason, a new dad of a seven-month-old, finally told his wife that there was a reason he was no longer touching her breasts during sex. "I can't stop thinking that [her breasts] are where my son gets his food," Jason admitted. Most husbands, though, wouldn't care if your chest suddenly produced soft-serve ice cream. They also usually enjoy the fact that you've gone up a cup size or two.

Mojo Makeover: For those of you who simply feel "touched out," as Tracy put it, consider introducing the bottle early (filled with pumped breast milk or formula). Doing so will free your body from constant use and possibly perk up your interest in hitting the sheets.

And if your husband is among those who have been surprised by an eyeful of milk, try feeding the baby right before you commence sex. That will reduce the chances of your leaking or spraying.

I'll probably be called on the carpet by breast-feeding advocacy groups out there, but truly, I think nursing is a splendid endeavor, well worth the many inconveniences and sacrifices. Still, if breast-feeding is truly putting the kibosh on your sex life, you may want to consider adding a bottle of formula to your daily regime. This will probably both kick-start your ovaries again and diminish the desire-bashing hormones raging around in your body.

Ann B. quit breast-feeding exclusively after six months because her sex drive had taken such a nosedive. "When I became pregnant, my mom drilled it into me that we needed to keep our marriage a priority, citing the fact that she and my dad focused too much on us, which was a contributing factor to the end of their marriage," she said. "So after I had the baby, I watched closely to make sure that Dan and I were still connected. Breast-feeding was great, but it rendered me completely not in the mood, all the time. I wanted to feel that connection with Dan again, so I quit nursing. Many people would say I was being a bad mother, but I was doing what was best for the whole family."

Allie, a vibrant and sparkly woman with three kids, also reported that her libido diminished drastically as a result of breast-feeding. After nursing Evie, her last baby, for over a year, she's seriously considering giving it up for the sake of her love life. "It's so frustrating because I feel totally passionless, and Pete says I have become radically different from the girl he married," she said.

It's a choice you have to make.

6. CHANCES ARE EXCELLENT YOU DON'T WANT TO GIVE BIRTH AGAIN SOON

On top of everything else, the thought of another pregnancy may be overwhelming enough to dampen your enthusiasm for sex. For greater freedom of mind, give some serious thought to birth control. There's a good chance you'll ovulate before you get your first period—something you might want to bear in mind if you're not exactly eager to see the pregnancy test come back positive again just yet.

7. YOU'RE STRESSED OUT

Nothing is more stressful than a colicky baby screaming bloody murder for hours while his frazzled parents try to calm him down. Throw in sleep deprivation, and you're going to be a bit of a basket case. Even if you have a baby who sleeps relatively well and isn't a yeller, adjusting to his or her presence in your life is plenty to deal with. On top of routine housework, a baby adds new feeding, changing, laundering, and bathing duties. And if your husband isn't pitching in with the chores, you probably resent him to some extent. (More on this in chapter 7.)

It's easy to be burned out by the end of the day, to be utterly depleted by meeting the ceaseless wants and needs of our little ones. "The biggest problem for me," says Lisa H., "is the perception that everyone wants something from me—my kids, my work and clients, my extended family, and my spouse."

"The last thing I wanted to think about when my husband came home was sex," my friend Kelly admitted. "The last thing I wanted [at the end of the day] was to satisfy someone else's needs, never mind my own." I imagine we moms can all relate. If we don't get in our heads that we need to be sexually active for our own sake, too, engaging in nooky will seem like just one more chore added to the pile.

Obviously, when you're harried and stressed, you don't feel sexy. I certainly didn't when I was cooped up for two or three months under gray winter skies with a baby who liked to let loose, bansheelike, on a regular basis. His crying made me feel frayed and unsettled, just the combination to lead me to my pals Ben and Jerry. And of course stress-eating just exacerbates body-image issues, which we'll get into in chapter 6.

Further shredding your nerves is the physiological reality of your body's stress response. In the postpartum period, your body's progesterone-like steroids, manufactured in big quantities during pregnancy, dwindle away to nothing. Since these natural substances are similar to anti-anxiety medicines, your mood may suffer the consequences.

Unfortunately, I have more bad news: When you are stressed, your body manufactures prolactin, the breast-feeding hormone. Just what you need: more shots of that notorious lust buster!

Mojo Makeover: For me, sensuality almost always unfolds in a relaxed atmosphere, not when I've just refereed a fractious sibling smackdown, soothed a toddler's tantrum, or cleaned poop from under my fingernails after a diaper detonation. Tune in to your body's stress level. Then try deep breathing (it works in the moment), running up and down the stairs, or a bubble bath to glue yourself back together.

8. YOU FEEL FAT

Your sister-in-law came home in her prepartum jeans (how, oh how, is that possible?), and even she isn't too jazzed about her après-baby bod. Our bodies have changed. No doubt about it. In this age that worships Britney-like abs, soft bellies and purple stretch marks can be quite dismaying. And women as a rule are unlikely to feel very amorous if they themselves feel unsexy. Experts say, though, that hardly any men are actually turned off by their wife's postchildbirth body.

Mojo Makeover: Tell your partner how you feel about your

extra pounds and the fact that your once-taut stomach is now quivering like a bowl of Jell-O. "I just feel as if I must be unappealing to you, which is making me less inclined to go for it again," you could say by way of a conversation starter.

You'll probably be surprised by how accepting he is of your new shape. Accept his compliments as sincere and believe that the sexual attraction between you doesn't depend on a perfect physique. Sneak in some exercise whenever you can. Slowly but surely the extra inches will come off, and the simple act of moving your body may make you feel better about yourself.

9. PPD Is Your Unwelcome Companion

"So what you're saying is, you're breast-feeding, you have postpartum depression, and you're taking Zoloft?" my friend Lisa H. said wryly. "I guess Doyle's totally out of luck, huh?" Well, the man certainly wasn't as lucky as he could have been, that's for sure. Postpartum depression (PPD) affects one in five women who have delivered a baby. In addition to decreased sex drive, PPD symptoms include a loss of appetite, difficulty sleeping, and an inability to enjoy the baby or other things that ordinarily give you pleasure. After I had my second baby, I felt overwhelmed, sad, irritable, and, yes, kind of frigid much of the time. Thankfully, PPD is highly treatable, but you have to open your mouth and ask for help, something that trips up a surprising number of women. (I address

PPD at length in *O for a Thousand Nights to Sleep,* my book about baby's first year.)

Mojo Makeover: Though usually curable, PPD won't go away if you don't seek treatment. Ask your doc about your best options—and be sure to ask for meds that won't further mess up your libido. This may require a period of trial and error under your doctor's supervision. Commonly prescribed antidepressants Prozac, Paxil, and Zoloft have been shown to dampen any glowing embers that haven't already been stomped out by the previously mentioned items on this list of libido busters. (Yikes!) I switched to medication that didn't make me gain weight (some meds do) or make me cold where I should have at least been warm, and it did make a real difference. I'm not saying I metamorphosed into some kind of tiger in the bedroom as soon as I took care of my PPD, but I did regain a certain bounce in my step, and the thought of having sex was no longer repulsive to me. Hey, it was a start!

Sparkplugs:
Five for the Drive

Amy Q., young mom of five munchkins and a pro at balancing passion and motherhood, sent along her top-five list of ways to make her hubby smile. "I like these because, when I am in the mood, I can make him feel blessed," she said, "and we both enjoy it!"

1. Make a trail of Hershey's Kisses up to the bed, where you are waiting for him when he gets home from work. (In Amy's house this only works if the five kids are at Grandma's or a friend's house!)

2. Play "Strip Go Fish"—or whatever card game works for you.

3. Come to bed with *nada* on.

4. Bring out the massage oil for a rubdown before bedtime.

5. Join him for his morning shower before he even realizes you're awake.

FIVE

Hollywood Moms and Real Red-Hot Mamas

Beating the Libido Busters, Part 2:
The Influence of Pop Culture

As the weeks wore on and the Arbuckle family settled into something of a routine, Debra found herself warming up again to the idea of lovemaking. Truth be told, Deb was in the mood far more often than she let Trevor know. Her sleep-deprived nights were becoming a thing of the past, and she had much more energy now. But somehow it felt strange to initiate sex. After all, she was a mom, and moms are not exactly known for being aggressive in the bedroom. Besides, Deb still carried an extra twenty pounds since having Micah. She wasn't too sure Trevor even found her all that tempting anymore anyway.

Though she was unaware of it, Debra's reticence about initiating sex was largely influenced by the messages of pop culture, which often rule the roost—and the bedroom. Like it or not, we are all products of our culture. Deeply informed to our very core by our society's views, we often adopt various viewpoints without even knowing where they came from. Sex is, it goes without saying, one area where we are profoundly influenced.

Western culture is most decidedly transfixed by all things sexy and sexual. This obsession shows up in advertisements, song lyrics, magazines, and on the Web. It even saturates prime-time television's so-called family hour. Since the sexual revolution of the previous century, talking about and depicting sensuality in all its many forms has become commonplace. Whereas the ladies' periodicals of the fifties promised articles about cooking, cleaning, and child rearing, today you can't buy a stick of gum without magazine covers yelling out at you, "Rock his world with these moves tonight!" and "Find your G spot in ten easy steps." Sex, or your lack of it, is a matter to be confronted daily.

See, on the surface, it appears we are completely fascinated with sex, but the reality is very different. Married couples have sex, on average, about once a week—so we're not exactly wearing out the bedsprings here in our nooky-crazed nation. Why in the world are we not making love with our mates on a regular basis?

Researchers say there are many physical causes for sexual dysfunction, such as painful intercourse and premature ejaculation, but by and large, as far as I can tell, the leading culprit seems to be a lack of libido, a general disinterest in sex. I think our society's very obsession may itself be a reaction to the absence of satisfying sex in our own lives. We're not actually doing it much, but we sure seem to want to read about it and watch it on television and in movies.

❧ THE SEXUAL REVOLUTION CONFUSION

What is the reason for this gap? During the last fifty or so years, cultural and marital attitudes toward sex have made dramatic shifts. In our grandparents' era, sex was viewed basically as a wifely obligation along with vacuuming and dusting. Generally speaking, it was assumed that husbands were entitled to sex, and wives "gave" it more from duty than from desire. (Of course, what transpired behind closed doors was probably a different story for many couples.) In the 1960s and 1970s, with the revolutions of feminism and sexuality, married sex was scrutinized and deemed a bore; today it's in as long as both husband and wife are equally swept away by passion.

Writer Caitlin Flanagan, in an astute *Atlantic* piece called "The Wifely Duty," reflected upon the cultural ideas that mold the way we conduct our intimate lives: "To many contemporary women… the notion that sex might have any function other than personal fulfillment (and the occasional bit of carefully scheduled baby making) is a violation of the very tenets of the sexual revolution that so deeply shaped their attitudes on such matters."[1]

Even if you have never thought of yourself as a feminist, you've still been affected by the ideas and changes wrought by that cultural insurrection. Our ideas and expectations of men and women and their roles have been altered, whether or not we wanted them to. Today's mothers are far more likely to work outside the home, even part time. And we expect much more from our mates as far as divvying up household and child-rearing chores. Any idea that sex is a burden we must bear to be good wives went the way of the floor polisher. (Oh, there are a few exceptions. Unfortunately, this notion still rears its head in some frigid circles.)

To further complicate matters, the cultural ideas of the sexual revolution tended to clash with religious ideals, which were evolving at a different pace and in a different direction. Consider the ideological brawl, now thirty some years past, among feminists, conservative Christians, and Christian writer Marabel Morgan, who wrote the iconic little book *The Total Woman* in the early seventies. Among her suggestions, Morgan urged her readers to show up at the door to greet hubby wearing nothing but Saran Wrap. (I've always wondered where the children of the home were at this point.) She suggested that wives who gave their man "super sex," using such techniques as moaning during lovemaking, could receive dividends like a new refrigerator. Feminists were outraged by the supposition that women were to be their husband's "sex slaves," and conservative elements of Christianity were miffed that Morgan was so frank about sexuality. My dad, a Christian book-seller, told me that some of his customers at the time were angry with him for not storing Morgan's book—"Christian pornogra-phy," they called it—in the back room somewhere as opposed to displaying it right there on the shelves where everyone could see it.

At any rate, a couple of big cultural motifs were forged during the seventies, just about the time many of today's young mothers were coming into the world. For one, the feminists got across the point that women, married or not, shouldn't have to "put out" if they didn't want to. Even if a woman was to stay at home and con-tinue with the traditional housework and child rearing—not her sole option, mind you—sexual performance was no longer one of her required duties. Second, solidified by Morgan despite conserva-tives' best efforts, was the notion that Christian women are sexual beings, and could—and should—keep the home fires sizzling by celebrating their sexuality. You don't have to put out, but you should want to put out.

So, in recap, our generation of women is expected to care for children and home—ideally with help from the man of the house—and very possibly work outside the home. At the very least she is expected to use her education, perhaps in volunteer work or homeschooling. Bottom line? We're plumb tuckered out. There's no way our generation can, as Morgan suggested, complete all housework by noon so that we can bathe and nap in the afternoon in order to conserve energy for "super sex."

Not surprisingly, then, it's been said that sleep is the new sex. With all the demands on us as mothers, wives, home managers, and possibly workers, it's all we can do to get the bare minimum of our to-do list done before collapsing in a heap somewhere. We as a culture crave shuteye as never before. "After working all day outside of the home, juggling dinner and the house, making time for my hubby and son—I just want to crawl in bed at the end of the day," says my friend Twila.

Remember that television jingle from the eighties for the perfume Enjoli? "I can bring home the bacon, fry it up in a pan, and never let you forget you're a man." That about sums up society's expectations of us and our own expectations of ourselves. Never mind that we are too exhausted to fry much of anything in a pan, although we feel guilty that we don't. The point of the advertising campaign was that we still need to be tigers in the bedroom even if we've worked all day and then fixed dinner and managed all matter of domestic endeavors. Tigers? *Grrrrr.*

Somehow, today's educated, career-savvy moms are supposed to do quite a bit with their days. We are also expected to be sexy and to want sex because, after all, we are no longer repressed and frigid! The only problem with these expectations is that we don't have any energy for nooky. And then we feel guilty for that, too, because everyone knows we should have a fantastic sex life, right?

It's enough to prompt a call to the local convent to see whether they have any openings for tired soccer moms.

❁ THE DISH: "HOLLYWOOD HASN'T GOT A CLUE"

As a generation, we are significantly influenced by movies, television, and music. And as a cultural indicator, Hollywood in particular is obsessed with sex. However, the kinds of messages the entertainment industry sends out are more hopelessly jumbled than ever.

On one hand, it's hard to escape the key point of sexual imagery in songs, movies, and ads: Sex is incredibly important, and having lots of it is essential to happiness. On the other hand, virtually all of the hanky-panky we see or hear about involves the young, single, and newly in love.

Apparently Hollywood doesn't think married sex is even worth mentioning. It's a fact that television shows depict sex between unmarried partners twenty-four times more frequently than between married partners.[2] "Movies, novels, and television shows almost never depict loving, responsible, devoted mothers as sexually active and assertive," writes Dr. Raskin. "One doesn't associate 'sexy' with 'soccer mom.' Who makes out in the back seat of a mini-van?"[3]

Pull up a chair for a little informal panel discussion on pop culture, sexuality, and motherhood. I'm sure you'll see what quickly became clear to me—how very much these mothers were affected by the media around them. Once they started thinking about how their perceptions were skewed by Hollywood, they really let loose. Maybe their rantings and ravings will help you recognize how you, too, have been affected by media images and messages.

"Motherhood in the media is one big airbrushed picture!" Margaret, mother of three, blasted. "Let's face it. How many 'mommy cams' do you see? Many people nowadays don't learn culture from their world. They copy culture from television, and stretch marks don't sell! Until these up-and-coming generations realize that mothering is a beautiful act in and of itself, our longing for 'reality mom' will be left behind closed doors." (About five minutes after Margaret uttered these words, the Fox network came out with the degrading and just plain icky reality show *The Swan*, in which average-looking women are "made over" by a team of plastic surgeons, personal trainers, and life coaches. So much for "reality mom"!)

For Lisa B., the incessant cultural 411—that everyone is getting it on, at least everyone except her—has led to feelings of guilt. She feels inferior to the sexy couplings portrayed by Hollywood because, as she says, "I start to think we're not having enough, so something's wrong with us. That something's wrong with me because I'm not (a) luring my husband to bed on a regular basis and (b) he's not luring me. It takes constant self-talk (and talk with my hubby) to confirm that [our sexual slump due to a new baby] is just a stage! It's during times like this that I'm very, very thankful for our committed, loving marriage!"

Several women in this group remarked on how their favorite television comedies underscore some element of their ideas about sexuality. "The perception is that everybody is doing it all the time, which statistically of course is a *huge* myth," Lisa H. said. "I do appreciate the show *Everybody Loves Raymond* for this reason." Though everybody may love Ray, including his wife, the guy doesn't get a whole lotta lovin'.

Neither does Jim, the buffoonish character played by Jim Belushi in the ABC comedy *According to Jim*. "I consider that show to be pretty realistic," says Ann, mother of a two-year-old. "The husband/father Jim wants to have sex any night he can, and the wife/mother wants to participate about 25 percent of the time. Pretty authentic odds to me!"

Still, the messages delivered by these shows are unsurprisingly mixed. "In *Everybody Loves Raymond,* wife Debra is thin and pretty, of course, but she also never wants to have sex because she's too tired or feels like reading a book," Joy commented. "That just underlines the message that moms aren't sexual beings."

And what about the fact that as a group television moms (post-Roseanne, anyway) are likely to be significantly hotter than their husbands? Let's face it, the husbands on *Raymond, Still Standing,* and other programs are not going to make anyone weak in the knees. But their wives, they of the taut abs and perfectly coifed hair and fashionable clothes, could easily turn heads wherever they go.

This fact didn't escape the attention of Mary, a mother of two small children. "Television shows me that somehow moms are extremely attractive (thin in particular) and sexy after all their years of marriage and kids."

What's the news flash embedded in the hot wife/average Joe package? That it's not okay to be a size 12, perfectly normal-looking woman even after you've had kids. This cultural message puts a lot of pressure on mothers to measure up bodywise. "Television moms always have makeup on, and their hair is looking perfect," Amy chimed in. "That never happens here! I just laugh now when things are getting steamy and my hair gets in the way. By the way, candlelight is very flattering even if you don't feel exactly perfect."

And there's more than television eating us up. Even if we don't subscribe to *People* or *Us* magazines, we are admittedly fascinated with the glowing glitterati and their beautiful, stylish journeys to parenthood.

"When it comes to movies and television and commercials, I can definitely say that there's very little overlapping of motherhood and sexuality. Both are portrayed, but not simultaneously," says Erika. "One exception to this may be the public's interest in famous women getting pregnant and having babies—Cindy Crawford, Sarah Jessica Parker, Kate Hudson, and Gwyneth Paltrow, to name a few recent ones. It seems that these women are able to have chil-

dren yet still maintain their sex appeal. This isn't necessarily helpful, though, because then you get into the whole issue of insane
expectations of what a sexy mom looks like."

True, television mothers seem to have a real knack for shedding
that baby weight in a hurry. They'll deliver their babies on one
week's episode (sometimes in a taxicab or hospital elevator), and by
the next week they will be as toned and taut as if they had spent
the last few months in intensive Pilates training rather than getting
huge and giving birth. We know that these women have personal
trainers who come to their homes, put them through their paces,
and whip into shape any flab they may have accumulated. They
also have nannies who can watch their babies when they're at the
gym. Sarah Jessica Parker, for one, has admitted that she wouldn't
have gotten so fit so fast after having her son had she not this kind
of help and support. But even when we know in our heads that
these star mamas have way more help than we do, their flat tum-
mies and buffed quads can nonetheless make us feel subpar about
our own shapes.

For Johana, though, these well-known *madres* have modeled
for her the fact that sexiness and mothering are not mutually exclusive. "Hollywood moms like Cindy Crawford and Madonna and
Demi Moore have shown that you can be sexy after becoming a
mom," she says. "I hope that's true because I'm clinging to that."

Still, this freelance model experienced firsthand the conven-
tional ideas about mothers and how they should look: "Recently I

went to San Francisco for a bachelorette party of a friend from high school. I was the only married woman there and the only mom. I hadn't seen the other women in eight years. We went out with the bride-to-be and wore our party pants. I was able to squeeze into pleather snakeskin pants and black tank and heels, which I thought was pretty good for having had a baby! One girl commented, which ticked me off, that I looked good 'for being a mom.' I couldn't help myself from replying, 'You look great too—for being an engineer!'"

Even in her pleather pants, Johana was judged through the lens of what people expect a mother to look like.

❀ "I Can't Be Sexy; I'm a Mom Now!"

It all boils down to this: soaking in all of these cultural news flashes over the whole of our lives has hugely affected our views of sex and motherhood, especially in the following three areas.

1. You Feel Weird Being Sexy—You're Someone's Mother for Crying Out Loud!

"Having a baby underscores the difference between having sex for pleasure and having sex for reproduction," says Dr. Raskin. "[After] you have a baby, your purpose is most likely to be pleasure—and therein lies the problem. Most moms have such a strong sense of maternal responsibility that doing something purely for their own physical pleasure can seem self-indulgent or greedy."[4]

We all have cultural snapshots in our brains that depict what is "appropriately" sexual and what isn't. Good moms, we think, certainly don't actually *want* sex or take the time to cultivate their sexuality. Do they? "My word!" the Good Mommy in our head lectures. "Isn't there some baby-related duty I must attend to—sterilizing, hand laundering, growing carrots in the backyard for organic baby food?—instead of satisfying my physical desires?" Focusing on our sexuality feels wanton, permissive, even unseemly—not at all how Good Mommy conducts herself.

2. You Don't Feel Entitled to Sex

Now that I have kids, the words of David Letterman's mom have echoed in my head many a time as I've wiped noses, packed lunches, changed diapers, folded clothes, and picked up probably thousands upon thousands of toys. We do and do until we can't do anymore! Putting sex, which is ideally a highly pleasurable activity, higher up on our priority lists can seem like a selfish thing to do. Crazy as it sounds, many moms feel guilty for "indulging" in anything—going out for coffee with a friend, seeing a movie they want to see, or, in this case, having sex. After Baby arrives, the mattress mambo becomes an impractical endeavor because there's no "useful" reason to do it. It takes a while for new moms to sort through these cultural messages as well as their new and strangely guilty response to doing anything—anything!—for themselves. Isn't a mom supposed to sacrifice herself to the point of sainthood, at which point she gets nominated to be on Oprah and win a week at the spa? Sometimes we really do believe that, don't we?

3. You Can't Shift Gears from Mommy Mode to Sexy Siren

Don't I know it can be tough switching from the role of parent to lover? After listening to Elmo, Winnie-the-Pooh, and who-have-you on television, in the movies, and on kid CDs, playing peekaboo in the bathtub, kissing any number of ouchies, and scraping hardened baby formula off your best stay-at-home-mom sweats, you hardly feel sexual. Asexual is more accurate, like some kind of robot/vegetable combo.

So it pays big to intentionally make the transition from frenzied caregiver to real woman. My friend Marisol, a mother of three under five and a part-time Spanish teacher, said one of her biggest hurdles was figuring out the whole "Can moms be sexy?" thing. "Marital lust is difficult because the unknown and forbidden that was present during dating is now known. To create [desire], there have to be intentional acts of 'naughtiness.' Kids are usually the main problem. You don't feel like being a sex kitten with a kid on your hips!"

✿ Mojo Makeover: Banish Those Lies

Permit Passion

The best moms soon figure out that they must practice self-care and intentionally nurture their love life in order to experience optimum balance and joy. "Try to consciously give yourself permission to indulge in things that make you feel good—a massage, a long walk, or a carefree roll in the hay with your partner," Dr. Raskin says.[5]

Cut the Martyr Act

Until we stop making martyrs of ourselves for the sake of our kids, we are unlikely to boost our sexual desire. We need to create balance in our lives; we need to carve out time for self-care if we are to know optimum mothering joy. In fact, as I hope I've emphasized clearly by now, we are not just *entitled* to a good romp in the hay once or twice a week; we *need* to have sex for our own well-being and for the well-being of our marriage and family.

Transition Well

Ann has enlisted her husband's help in making the transition from her role as mom to her role as attractive, desirable, and downright sexy wife: "Dan and I have had a number of discussions about what helps to make for a good transition time, and we decided this was best done after dinner," she says. "Making time to have coffee/tea/dessert and catch up with each other is vital. Spending time talking with each other helps us reconnect and get the details of life out of our systems." What works in your home? Maybe hubby can give the kids a bath while you unwind. Knowing the goal, chances are he'll readily agree.

Changing how you refer to your mate can also help move things along. Try calling each other by pet names: "Oh, by the way, lover boy, Buford Jr. puked all over the hallway" and "What do want for dinner, sweet cheeks?" That kind of thing. Refrain, if you will, from referring to your spouse as Daddy when the kids are not directly involved. (I know of a couple who call each other Mama and Papa all the time even though their children have been out of the house for over a decade. I also happen to know they have sex once a year. Why once a year? Only they know, and I ain't gonna ask! Call me crazy, but I'm pretty sure there's a connection.)

Consciously Disregard

I was particularly inspired by Emily, mom to a toddler with one bambino bun in the oven. She intentionally disregards the perfect standards set forth in movies, television, and magazines. "I don't feel pressured by society's obvious message that sex is for the young and beautiful. I think sex is much more about relationship, sacrifice, and confidence," she says. "I find that when I read lowbrow fashion magazines, I feel bad about myself and my sexuality. Who can compare themselves to an unattainable, airbrushed model? My best method for staying confident and feeling sexy is to listen to my husband and what he says and feels."

Sparkplugs: They Snooze, You Win

Okay, twenty-first-century wonder moms: when swimming upstream against the cultural currents, take advantage of any opportunities you and your husband can find to strengthen your bond—like while the kids are snoozing. Unlike the strength-sapping cultural messages, finding what works for you will renew your energy for the long haul. My Dish moms throw out a few lifesavers:

- "Our daughter is still not a very good sleeper, even at one, so we have to try to fit in a burst of passion when she's actually asleep. On Friday nights, when she goes down at seven thirty, we spring into action. Whoever's not putting her down that night is in charge of getting the fire going, laying down some blankets in front of the fireplace, dimming the lights, lighting the candles, choosing a romantic CD. Most times I will have made some kind of dessert, or Phil will pick up something on his way home from work. We usually have a few hours before Tori wakes up, so we can relax and unwind.

There's no pressure exactly to have sex, but I can't think of a time when this has not happened! It doesn't happen every single Friday, but when we are planning it, I look forward to it all week." —Tracy

- If your kids are old enough, pitch a tent in the backyard for them to have a sleepover. Maybe having an older cousin sleep with them would give you more peace of mind. At any rate, if the kids are in a tent, you and your mate can do whatever you like without the threat of a break-in (or at least you'd have more warning than you usually do).

- "Every Saturday afternoon we have mandatory naptime for everyone in the house, including my husband and me. That way, when the kids go to sleep that night, we actually have energy to enjoy a special evening together instead of wiping out at eight as usual." —Vicki

- "Our parents both live out of town, so we don't go out too often. It's more economical and easier to just create a special evening at home when our son is asleep. I've been getting a prepared meal for two from the deli at our grocery store for these nights. I just heat up the food, and we eat a peaceful, companionable, nice meal. I try to clear out all the toys and things on the floor, and I put a fresh tablecloth on the table to make the atmosphere more inviting. I'll put on makeup and nicer clothes, too, even though it's tempting to just wear the old sweatshirt with the baby food stains on it! Mike takes a shower, and he looks pretty hot too. It's not as good as actually going out, but it is the next best thing!" —Jennie

- "I have two words for sparks and romance: tether dates! (Don't run to Dr. Phil. I came up with this one on my own.) For those who have not caught a single episode of *COPS* in the last fifteen years, a tether is an electronic device that is secured around a person's ankle to monitor their whereabouts when under house arrest. Now, house arrest may be strong words for parents of small children, but let's be real—we ain't going nowhere! My husband and I do get out quite often and have a warden, I mean baby-sitter, come watch the kids. But those long weekdays and weekends when the baby-sitter is busy require a tether date. A tether date must happen when the kids have had no nap and can realistically hit the sack earlier. Turn off the television, the phones, the fax, the computer, the satellite tracking device, and focus on each other. Eat some cheese without wrappers and drink a beverage without a straw! Create a calm atmosphere where you and your spouse can just be with each other. Even if you sit in silence at first, you need to have this designated space in your week 'just for us' because when the candles are snuffed, it's back to reality!" —Margaret

- "If we really need to have a private night, we sometimes let the kids camp out in a tent in the playroom, with sleeping bags and snacks and a longish movie. It usually takes a while for them to settle in and figure out they can't come and bother us, but when they do, it's as good as if we've gotten a baby-sitter for the night. I'll cook a meal that is decidedly not kid-friendly—like mussels or something— and the two of us will have a quiet, unhurried meal. Then we'll snuggle up on the couch and pop in a movie of our own, something the kids would definitely not be interested in seeing. Once in a while the kids will start fighting, and we'll have to break it up, but they usually leave us alone. I think they know they've got it good with the snacks and movie and tent, and they would rather not return to their usual beds!" —Monica

SIX

You've Got a Body Even a Mother Can Love... and in a Thong Too

Beating the Libido Busters, Part 3:
Body Image

As Trevor and Deb's sixth anniversary approached, Trevor began to desperately yearn for more sensuality, intimacy, physical closeness, and connection with his wife. How could they once again get to the place they were last year, when they had found their way back to each other as a couple? Trevor had no idea. He felt hurt, angry, devalued, and frustrated, and he gradually stopped investing his heart and soul in their relationship. *If she wants us to be roommates—fine!* he thought. *Then that's what we'll be.*

Debra, meanwhile, could not put her finger on what was happening to her marriage. All she knew was that Trevor was gone all the time, either working, golfing, or attending a church event. When he was home, he was attentive to the kids, but he seemed to treat her as a nanny or a coworker—politely and without affection. The more he distanced himself, the less attractive she felt and the less inclined she was to be touched or kissed. Debra was battling some insecurities about her body as it was. Trevor's coldness—for that's what she felt his attitude was—only made her feel more unappealing.

Her sister, then a freshman in college, teased Debra that she dressed like their mother. If the two sisters ever went shopping together, Debra was embarrassed by the fact that she was a good thirty pounds heavier than she used to be, and that much plus ten pounds more than her skinny, cute sister. She felt sure everyone compared them and thought, "Thin sister, jumbo sister." Her anxieties about her weight only stressed her out, which led to Oreo binges when Avery and Micah were napping.

But when Debra's doctor told her to lose weight, she took it as a wake-up call. Even if she'd never be model-thin like her sister, Debra was suddenly motivated to become healthy again—if not for her sake, then for her kids.

❧ EMBRACING OUR BOTTICELLI BODIES

Tell the truth now: you didn't wake up this morning thinking, "Oh what a beautiful build I have! This bod not only brought a child into this world, but it's positively replete with lush curves, like a Botticelli angel!"

I would guess your self-talk regarding your figure is more along these lines: "I have a fat derriére, and my thighs are total saddlebags, and my abs? Let's not even go there. I always thought I had a pretty toned tummy, but since having kids, it's practically fallen to the floor. Along with my breasts…"

There's nothing like motherhood to induce severe body-image anxiety in a woman. And there's nothing like feeling crummy about your shape to induce a severe lack of interest in getting naked. In a study published in the *Journal of Obstetrics and Gynecology*, Dr. Rosemary Basson wrote, "In my interviews with female patients, 80 percent comment that their feelings about weight interfere with their sexual abandon or make them feel self-conscious."[1]

There are biological reasons for your blossoming figure, not that those reasons will make you feel less insecure about your changing shape. After having a baby, your metabolism is reduced by 15 to 25 percent—and dieting can make it drop even lower. According to Debra Waterhouse, author of *Outsmarting the Female Fat Cell After Pregnancy*, our fat cells dig in and resist with all their might our efforts to banish them. Sluggish metabolism? Stubborn fat cells? Kid-related stress leading to trips to the fridge? It's no wonder moms struggle so much with their weight...and their body image. Then, to add insult to injury, our attempts at slimming down often backfire. One Australian study found that new moms who dieted had greater body dissatisfaction than others. And the more dissatisfied you are with your body, the more likely you are to sabotage your efforts at weight loss.[2]

What I found most surprising—at least at first I was shocked—was that this life stage of mothering young children makes us more vulnerable to serious problems than even the teenage-girl population. "The University of Oxford in England found that pregnancy was one of the strongest life events to trigger an eating disorder," Waterhouse writes. "You may not have an eating disorder, but you may be a disordered eater, meaning you have an unhealthy relationship with food and your body."[3]

We may be grown, married women with mortgages and responsibilities, but most of us still haven't kicked the disgust for our bodies that we harbored as sixteen-year-olds. Of course, when we were sixteen, we had a turbocharged metabolism. Back in the day, we could down a deep-fried, sugarcoated anything and practically burn it off within an hour. And yet somehow we still obsessed about our "thick" legs!

Now we have much more working against us, physiologically and culturally, than we've ever had before. And somehow all this pressure seems par for the course. "We've matured into adults thinking that dieting, body satisfaction, and food fears are a normal part of being a woman," Waterhouse points out. "Well, there's nothing normal about waking up every morning hating your body, eating salad with fat-free dressing every day for lunch, or avoiding any event that calls for a bathing suit."[4]

There's also nothing normal about disliking your body so much that you dislike sex because it requires peeling off your clothes. After all, it's hard to get busy under the sheets when you're wearing footed pajamas. Lydia, for one, complained that her relentless dissatisfaction with her torso, trunk, and everyplace else was throwing a wrench into her bedroom life. "I am uncomfortable with the way I look and the weight I've gained since the girls came," she said. "My impulse is always to conceal my body, not flaunt it!" It's a fact that a whopping 96 percent of us women are less than thrilled with our physiques.[5] (Victoria's Secret models, professional tennis players, and your smug sister-in-law make up the other 4 percent.) Clearly, sex is between your ears, and body image is one glaring example of how your brain and your emotions can contribute to a low sex drive.

Experts contend that women who worry about their appearance may not only be less interested in sex but may even show less affection to their husband, which of course is not at all a good thing for closeness at any level.

Do you cringe when your husband touches you because you think he must be appalled by your flabbiness? Actually, study after study shows he couldn't care less. Men are generally much less critical and much more accepting of their partner's body than they're given credit for. Nothing is more captivating to a man than a woman who feels sexy and acts with sexual confidence, regardless of her perceived imperfections.

❀ Mojo Makeover, Part 1: Slim Down the Self-Deprecation

What can you do to build a healthy body image and captivate your man with wild abandon and reckless self-acceptance? Try these tips and see if you don't start feeling better about the frame you're in:

Think Positive

Start sending confidence-boosting messages to yourself about your sexuality. Some affirmations that can help are: "I love my body," "I love being touched and touching," and "I love to make love." Instead of constantly criticizing your shape, remind yourself of the positives: "I have great toned arms" or "My waist is really starting to whittle down lately." When you tell yourself ten times a day that your stomach is flabby or your ankles are thick, you start to believe it, so counteract these faultfinding little messages with some encouragement.

Ask the Right Questions

Resist the urge to ask your guy, "Do you think I'm fat?" The reason: self-deprecating put-downs might steer your husband toward thinking the very thing you fear. Instead, use a more straightforward approach. Ask, "How do I look?" with an air of confidence and a big smile. This approach will help ensure that your husband will like what he sees and tell you so.

Accept Your Husband's Compliments

Evelyn and her husband have a secret to building each other up. "We constantly tell each other, 'I love you' and 'Thank you for helping bring our daughter into the world.' My husband also tells me every day that he wants ten more children. I know he's not serious, but it makes me feel wanted, sexy, and appealing, and gradually all thoughts about stretch marks and the like fade away." Evelyn's onto something here. But for some of us, before our husbands will boost our spirits with encouraging words, we have to tell them that's what we want! We women are famous for expecting our guys to be mind readers when a little direction on our part is all that's needed. "You know, Harry, I haven't felt that upbeat about how I look since the baby came. It would help me a lot if you gave me some positive feedback about my body." Without this communiqué, your lover may even avoid complimenting you, sensing as he may that your physique is a touchy subject.

Move Your Body

You may loathe exercise, but it's key to feeling good about your shape. I go to the gym once or twice a week and work out on the elliptical machine for about forty-five minutes. I probably don't get my heart rate up enough to do much in the way of weight loss, but it does make me feel more toned and fit. I also try to work out with weights two or three times a week. Weight training is wonderful because you can do it at home with free weights, and experts say there's nothing like it for revving up your metabolism. A couple of weeks after I started, I noticed my legs and arms getting more muscular. This regime certainly didn't transform me into Gisele Bündchen, but I do feel great about my legs and arms! I admit, my little efforts are less than what the trainers at the gym would have me do, but it's something—and amazingly, something is all it has taken for me to feel that much better about my whole body.

Jaye was successful in her weight-loss efforts, and the result has tuned up the lovemaking engine in her marriage. "I feel much more attractive since I lost twenty pounds," she said. "I don't think Charlie wanted me any more or any less when I weighed more, but it makes me feel better about myself and more responsive to his moves. Also, I have definitely been more into wearing sexy under-wear and pajamas. I think, *These look good on me!*"

So You Dress Like a Mom, and Your Underwear Could Pass Inspection at an Amish Colony

How many of you still wear maternity underwear even though your child is now three? A quick show of hands, please. There, see, you raised your hand, and up until a few months ago, I would have raised mine too. I would have stood up at a meeting of sex-starved moms and said, "Hello, my name is Lori, and I wear dowdy under-wear." But today I can gladly say that I quit the utilitarian-panties habit cold turkey awhile back. Why? Because the more research I did on moms and sexuality, the more I realized that you have to feel sexy in order to act sexy.

Now listen up because I'm not saying that you should start wearing plunging necklines and miniskirts to the preschool picnic. What I am saying is that the act of choosing and wearing silky, lacy, pretty things no one knows about can revolutionize your self-image. You won't be revamping your underwear situation just for your husband either, although he'll go through his own little revo-lution of sorts, I'm sure. Wear some sexy undergarments for your-self and see what happens!

"Married women with kids—embrace the thong and say

good-bye to those granny panties!" says my friend Margaret. "Okay, maybe a thong is a big first step for you. If so, try a bikini cut! Throw away those time-of-the-month or pre/postpregnancy tighty whities! To weed out your collection, ask yourself, 'What undergarments of mine would I rip down immediately if they were hung on a clothesline on national television?' When we feel sexy, even in sweats, we stand taller, hug longer, and laugh louder. Even if you are the only one who knows you're wearing more lace than your dining room table, it does make a difference, and it will add some bounce to your step—at least, after you get used to the thong!"

What Smells So Heavenly?

Aromatherapy connoisseurs, perfumeries, and scientists all get behind the fact that certain scents can drive us wild with desire—or maybe just deliver a subtle little hint that a certain someone wants to get cozy. Spritz on a few of these luscious scents and see what develops:

- Vanilla and licorice are proven to make men melt like homemade ice cream on a sweltering summer day. Try Avon's Treselle or Crabtree & Evelyn's Savannah Gardens Eau de Toilette.

- Roses, the everlasting symbol of romance and sweetness, send this rosy message: "You, me, upstairs,

Did I mention that Margaret is the mother of three children under five? She's right on about the weeding out! If you knew that some stranger would be seeing you in your underwear, would yours embarrass you? (Why would that ever happen? you ask. Well, picture a college student in downtown Chicago, the Windy City, having her skirt blow up to her chin on a blustery fall day before a crowd of witnesses. These things can and do happen—to me at least!) That white cotton nursing bra (again, the baby stopped nursing years ago) and the unmatched, frayed panties would never suffice. You'd want your underwear to be presentable. Trust me. (Ask me about the time I had a car accident and woke up

---

behind locked doors, ASAP!" Try Givenchy's Very Irresistible.

- "Aruba, Jamaica, ooh I wanna take ya…" When sandy beaches and palm trees are far, far away, bring the hot notion of tropical mambos closer with the aphrodisiac fragrances of jasmine, white musk, and exotic flowers. Try Estée Lauder's Beyond Paradise, Calgon's Tropical Dream Intense, and Ralph Lauren's Blue.

- Fire up those pheromones with libido-invigorating citrus scents: Try Céline Dion's fragrance with orange blossoms.

---

looking into the eyes of a drop-dead hot physician. True story!) Yet for everyday use, *for our husbands,* we settle for the useful, the practical, and the frumpy, in both underwear and outerwear categories.

Let me insert a note here about modesty: the Bible is big on modesty; that is, on not flaunting our sexuality for the watching world. Again, I am not suggesting Christian women dress in tight leather skirts, midriff tops, and fishnet stockings. We have to be careful about how we present ourselves to men with whom we have not traded vows. This doesn't mean, though, that we have to cover every square inch of our bodies with fabric. Nobody says moms have to look and dress poky. Yet somehow the idea that it's unseemly or not worth our time to be sexy—even for our husband—creeps in, and the next thing you know, we've put the *matron* in *matronly.*

I'll never forget the Oprah episode about "getting in touch with your inner sexpot." Oprah and her team "made over" several women, all moms, each of whom had buried her sexuality beneath appliquéd cardigans. Appliquéd knit items, just so you know, are those sweaters and vests and cardigans that have cute little kittens and hearts and flowers pieced onto them. Many of these sweaters are worn seasonally, with apple patterns in September or candy canes at Christmas. You get the picture. One of Oprah's guinea pigs, a sweet young mother of about thirty, was wearing a cardigan covered in pumpkins. Adorable, Oprah pointed out, if you're seven...or seventy.

Get this: when the Pumpkin Lady emerged from her make-over, Oprah's stylists hadn't put her in fishnet stockings and a bustier. Instead they had given her contact lenses and some very moderate hair extensions, and they had clad her in a pretty, slightly body-conscious top and pants. She looked amazing, like a different woman, years younger and light-years sexier. Yet she wasn't wearing anything inappropriate or immodest. Then the housewife formerly known as Pumpkin Lady performed a little pole dance for her husband (and, it must be said, for ten million viewers), who was sitting in the audience. He was just agog. I thought the guy was going to need medical attention.

The young mom hadn't lost a pound or consulted a steamy, shrink-wrapped sex manual. She hadn't (as far as I know) resolved that her husband was more important than her children or even gotten up the guts to leave the kids for the night. But that young woman, who before her makeover looked for all the world like a sixty-year-old kindergarten teacher, discovered how to access the sensual, sexy mama beneath the appliqués.

You don't need a makeover from Oprah to accomplish the same thing. All you need is to give yourself permission to dress sexy, even if only you and maybe your man know you're dressed that way.

Saying that a change of underthings will magically rev up your sexual interest is flimsy, I agree. But flimsy can still work, especially when it comes to what we wear under our oh-so-appropriate soccer-mom duds. Take "Tales from the Love Shack: The Thong" near the end of this chapter as your inspiration. Or check out the true confessions of my Dish panel (below) as they blab about whether to thong or not to thong. (Now don't get scared off if you think wearing a thong is like having a pebble in your shoe all day. The panel had some alternate ideas and other suggestions for transforming your underduds.)

THE DISH: "NO GRANDMA UNDERWEAR HERE!"

"Hey, I'm all about Old Navy pj bottoms and a tank top," says Mary. "I like to use the excuse that I wouldn't want to get caught in my lingerie if we had a house fire. I mean, let's be practical!" And, yes, let's face it. Most nights are going to be about comfort and ease, not cramming our body parts into itchy lace and thongs.

There is a happy medium to be found, however, between a bustier and a stained T-shirt, between stiletto heels and bulky Winnie-the-Pooh sweats. Sometimes a little attention to sleepwear and undergarments can pay off in a big way.

"I have made an effort to ditch the granny panties in favor of more attractive undergarments," Ann says. "Even colored cotton bikini-style panties offer some allure, while still being pretty comfy. In the summer months I wear a lot of thong underwear, and Dan loves that. I find that wearing sexy underwear makes me feel a little sexy all day long." (Did ya get that? All day long!) "My favorite sleeping pj's tend to be of the cotton and flannel family," she admits. "I am continually on the hunt for attractive but comfortable and warm pj's. So far I have one pair of dark-purple satin pj's that Dan considers attractive and I consider comfortable."

Several women confessed that they rarely, if ever, grab a filmy, satiny something from their lingerie drawer because first, they can't get it open and second...well, why bother? At least that's Erika's mind-set. "Every night I climb into a pair of boxers and a T-shirt. I have a couple pieces of lingerie (from a lingerie shower before my wedding eight years ago!), but they always come off within seconds, so I fail to see the point of spiffing up my bedtime attire." Emily concurs: "My pajamas are definitely *not* sexy," she admits. "They do exist in my bedroom, but like most women, I don't wear them. For us, pomp and circumstance seems unnecessary. I think we both find a lingering kiss more romance-inducing than great pj's, although that never hurts. I sometimes get them out as a way of signaling the night's coming attractions. They are also fun to save for overnight getaways."

Emily's right. For some couples, lacy teddies and whatnot are redundant. Why go all out dressing up for sex when the garments will soon—hopefully—be flung across the room? My friend Kathy has great criteria for buying lingerie: "Easy on, easy off, looks good on the floor."

But for other duos, lacy camisoles and silky slips are just the thing to beguile and begin!

Ann again: "Here's the thing: I have a lovely array of what I refer to as 'recreational lingerie,' but I don't sleep in the stuff. It's for attraction and seduction, and it's rarely comfortable enough to sleep in," she says. "I do have one lace camisole and panty set that makes for nice summer pajamas."

Initially Tera offered just a glimpse of what was stoking her home fires. At first, her clothing report was brief. "I wear an orange Eddie Bauer T-shirt and shorts. Cute, but not particularly sexy," she says. "I used to have a cotton nightgown, but a certain man's hands kept seeking out my legs at night and finding that exciting. I also told my hubby that I needed to wear decent clothes to bed because I must be proper in front of my son in case he gets up at night!"

"Proper," she says. Hmm. Well, Tera might be proper most of the time, you know, just in case her son walks in or something (which is why God invented locks), but further digging—plus the knowledge that her mojo makeover story could help others—prompted Tera to tell all. "A few years ago, our sex life had been in the doldrums. I decided to get my hubby a special Christmas gift. I shopped at Victoria's Secret and got a jazzy little number that I could wear. Believe me, that present didn't go under the tree! Now, every year since, he expects that little gift of me-in-something-tiny and can't wait to see what the new one will be. This year I got some new see-through panties to wear in the weeks prior to Christmas. Kind of a preshow, I guess. Worked for us!"

But of all on my panties panel, no one put more thought into boudoir basics than Marisol. Of course, she's Latina, and you know what they say about Latin lovers! "The winter is when I go to bed looking the frumpiest," Marisol claims. (Read on and see that frumpy is the least of this hot mama's problems.) "I wear socks and pj pants, and I do try to wear a tight white T-shirt so he can see my goods, but I'm still warm." Warm is good. "Goods" are good too. "When we were first married, I slept in the nude because that's what John preferred. And I didn't mind. But when we had our first baby, I got into the habit of wearing tight tanks when I was nursing to hold everything in. Now that my kids are past the nursing stage, I do have a special drawer for fun lingerie. I put them on for our in-house dates, but once the hot sex is over, I slip back into my tank and bikinis. No grandma underwear here. Well, okay, maybe one pair is kind of gramma-ish."

Marisol's final point underscores the importance of tapping our femininity and sensuality: "It's interesting that ever since I went on a girlfriends' reunion in Miami Beach, my underwear has also changed. I noticed then that I wasn't in touch with my feminine power. I started wearing thongs and lace briefs. They are now part of my normal 'unmentionables' collection."

Debra Takes the Plunge

Debra stuck with her intent to improve her attitude about self-care. She got a jogging stroller and ran with Micah while Avery stayed with Trevor or Grandma. The exercise was hard, but meeting her running goals gave her an amazing feeling of accomplishment. By the time Micah was a year old, Debra was thinking about entering a 5K in their city. She felt healthier than she had since Avery was born more than three years earlier.

Shopping trips with her sister became less and less the torturous endeavors they once were. Deb started buying more fashionable, body-conscious clothes that were better suited to her still-young age than the frumpy, baggy stuff she had been wearing.

When her neighbor had an in-home lingerie party, Debra felt obligated to go because the hostess, Abby, had attended Debra's candle party. Reluctantly, she sat through the presentation of lacy teddies, camisoles, and panties. But soon she found herself getting caught up in the spirit of the evening. *Trevor would like that little number,* she thought to herself about a black and red see-through outfit. *Wouldn't he be shocked if I went to bed in that thing?*

Well, Debra had to buy something because that's how these parties work, after all. Her neighbor had bought a ridiculously expensive candle at Deb's party that would probably last her for five years, it was so huge. Deb felt she had to buy more than a sachet of lavender!

The wheels in her mind started turning. Wouldn't Trevor be freaked if she put this outfit on? He was used to Deb wearing sweats to bed every night, and those hardly ever came off anymore.

Debra had been relieved, initially, when Trevor had stopped bugging her about having sex—frequent sex, that is. They still came together once every few weeks or so. But that was a few months ago, and she had been in a different frame of mind then. With the running and all, Deb had more energy and felt more confident about herself. Come to think of it, she missed sex! That realization did it. "I'll take it!" Debra said, more loudly than she had intended. Her friends laughed, and the party consultant grinned at her. "Your man can send me a thank-you note for hooking you up with this," she said.

An hour or so later, Debra was in the bathroom, wiggling herself into the red and black outfit. She was smiling to herself as she pictured Trevor's reaction. "Wanna see what I bought tonight?" she yelled. Trevor was reading a guitar magazine in bed. "Hmm? Okay, sure. Whatever," he said, distracted. A vague thought flitted through his mind: *Why would she have Tupperware in the bathroom?*

The bathroom door opened, and Debra came out. Trevor didn't look up from his magazine. "Aren't you gonna check it out?" she said playfully.

Trevor looked up. His first thought was *Who, oh who, is that woman standing in my bedroom?* His second thought was that Debra had not, evidently, gone to a Tupperware party.

"Whoa." It was all Trevor could manage between shock and budding desire.

"Do you like?" Debra asked cheekily, spinning around.

He liked. He definitely liked.

❀ MOJO MAKEOVER, PART 2: GET YOURSELF SOME VA-VA-VOOM!

Dump the frump, girlfriend. You can do it! I don't care how old you are or how much you weigh. Pretty clothes, underwear, and lingerie do come in your size! I truly believe that how we dress deeply influences our sense of self. If we walk around all our lives in pumpkin sweaters, wearing pragmatic bras and prosaic panties, covering ourselves like a bunch of nuns from head to toe, we will feel dowdy—on the inside and the outside. When we make changes to our clothes, even our underclothes, we make changes to our sense of sensuality. And when we feel sensual, we want to express that feeling, *capisce?*

A note to my practical readers: I know what you girls are thinking. You have enough sets of serviceable underwear to last you until the cows come home, so why spend a bunch of cash on new, frivolous sillies that serve no good purpose? Besides, you like comfort, and the panties you are currently wearing are as comfortable as those old sweats you've been wearing to bed since Clinton was in office. Why fix what ain't broke? Well, I'm here to tell you, my down-to-earth friend, you don't have to dent your wallet in order to refurbish your skivvies situation. And if you're so ferociously committed to being comfortable—well, we might still have a tip or two for you. Read on, O sensible one. Practicality and prettiness can coexist under your durable denims. And for the rest of you—those who enjoy daydreaming and imagining the possibilities as well as the starry-eyed who relish idealism, whimsy, and la-di-da—boy, do I have some fun assignments for you!

✿ DITCH THE MATERNITY UNDERWEAR

It's impossible to feel desirable when you're wearing billowy yards of viscose for no good reason. If your tyke is over the age of one, pack the mini-tents away for your next gestation. And if you're done having babies—for sure now—pack 'em away forever.

Take Inventory

What's in your drawer of unmentionables? Toss the frayed, the ripped, the holey pairs of panties that have seen brighter days. Replace them with appealing new ones in colors that make you feel attractive. Remember: Underwear is never just underwear. Black make you feel skinny? Rack up the black undies. Feel pretty in pink? Pink it is! Little touches like lace will go a long way in making you feel sexy. The point is, your underwear needs to reflect your femininity and sensuality.

What's in your closet? If it's lined with appliquéd cardigans, you probably aren't very happy with me right now. The thought of doing away with clothes that make you feel "sweet" and "safe" could be strange and uncomfortable. You'd probably feel much more comfortable hiding your sensuality forever under that adorable kitten sweater. (You do know, don't you, that cat earrings are just around the corner?) It's true that great underwear alone can make you feel like a new woman. But getting out of your comfort zone with the rest of your wardrobe is not such a bad thing. It can be energizing, liberating, and stretching. And I'm not actually suggesting you fill two paper sacks with all your knitwear festooned with puppies, apples, shamrocks, and Santas and donate it all henceforth to Goodwill. Even I'm more practical than that! We all need some comfy sweats, "fat" jeans, and other no-brainer clothes to slip into during the throes of PMS. But do consider your wardrobe. How much of your closet is stuffed with garments that hide your femininity? Is your wardrobe thirty years more dowdy than it should be? Do your clothes provide coverage suitable for the turn of the nineteenth century?

Like a new diet, you can gradually make different choices when you buy your clothes. Are your choices appealing? Do they reflect your femininity and age? You don't have to break the bank, either: While you're at Goodwill with your paper sacks, check out their racks for some nifty new duds. While on my anniversary weekend at Cocoa Cottage, we popped over to the local Goodwill for fun, and I found a gorgeous plum-colored cashmere (cashmere!) sweater for six dollars.

What do you sleep in? Okay, you are talking to the queen of polar-bear pajamas here. I love nothing more than to get cozy in one of my six pairs of flannel pj's, a cup of tea in one hand and an enthralling page-turner in the other. But I don't wear Nanook of the North every night. Not even close! Nor do I wear lacy see-through getups every night. Most nights I just wear something attractive and comfy. Target is great for pretty, soft, fun, and cheap sleepwear sets.

Usually, as Emily pointed out in her Dish comments, lingerie is redundant. I could be wearing my polar bears, and still we end up, um, hibernating. Naked does the trick too. Sometimes, however, a little more snap, crackle, and pop is in order. Is your lingerie drawer jammed because you haven't opened it for seven years? I must confess, most of my own seductive getups are dusty with disuse. Many of the pieces in my lingerie collection are size 8, which was what I was in college and thus the size my bridal-shower gifts came in. I'm no longer a size 8. But I have since made it a point to pick up a va-va-voom garment once a year or so. If it's been years since you shopped for a little something slinky, investigate the possibilities. Victoria's Secret a little too over-the-top for you? Try Gap Body. I love their underwear because it's comfortable, cute, and fits great. You don't have to buy a red and black lace bustier/thong torture device. Start slow and easy with a piece that makes you feel flirty and sensual. Kristina bought a size 14, soft yellow, two-piece tank and shorts set in a sumptuous, satiny fabric. It makes her feel beautiful and puts her in the mood for romance. And the best part: it's "easy on, easy off, looks good on the floor"!

Make the most of your purchase. Hide it. E-mail your husband and tell him you went shopping for lingerie. Drop hints about color and texture. Tantalize the man a little. You'll discover you can't wait to model it and see what develops.

Test Drive a Thong

If you haven't already tried wearing a thong, there's no time like the present. I do have thongs that are more comfortable than others, so don't base your evaluation solely on the time you wore one and it drove you crazy. Don't assume you're not a thong person. Maybe you are and you just don't know it! At any rate, three to five dollars is not too much of an investment, so if you hate it, you can just skip the thong and opt for choices that still make you feel sexy without bothering you. The lighter the fabric the better because you don't want to feel "cheeky" with heavy-duty cotton bunching up all day long. As you'll soon read in "Tales from the Love Shack," Lucy and her love life were transformed by this tiny scrap of fabric.

(The two other "Tales" in this book are about me, and I haven't even changed my name! This saga, though, has been cobbled together from a couple of true confessions told to me by shy Dish ladies who wished to remain anonymous. By the way, my own experiences have corroborated theirs, so it *could* be a tale from my own love shack. I'm not saying it is, but…oh, never mind! Just read it—and if the thong fits…)

TALES FROM THE LOVE SHACK: THE THONG

"One day I was totally out of underwear, and all I could find was this lace thong thing I had bought when we were first married. Or maybe Don bought it for me. It's hard to remember that far back. Well, I threw in a load of undies and put on the thong for the day. I must say, it wasn't the most comfortable thing I had ever worn, but maybe the discomfort was the very thing that reminded me I was wearing it. Here's the weird thing: I was aware that I had on a thong, and it began to change my perception of myself. The day at home was a vanilla day, not terrible and not fantastic. I had my share of fights to break up and spilled juice to mop up. But I still felt less…frumpy or something as I went through the day.

"When I took a shower, I put the thong back on and thought, 'I am a woman in a thong!' Then when Don called home from work, in the middle of telling him what he should pick up from the store on his way home, I said, 'Hey, honey, I'm wearing a thong.' There was this big pause on the other end, and he said, 'I beg your pardon?' We kind of snickered and hung up.

"It wasn't my imagination that he acted differently when he came home. When I was cooking dinner, he came up behind me and whispered, 'Hi there, thong girl.' I kind of giggled, and that kind of flirting went on all evening. When I was folding clothes, which included that batch of underwear, he grabbed my stack of panties and pretended to throw them away. 'You won't be needing these anymore,' he smirked. The funny thing was he hadn't even seen the thong. His imagination totally carried him away with the image.

"Well, by the time the kids were in bed, I felt pretty hot. I hopped into bed with the thong, skipping the Winnie-the-Pooh sleep shirt I had been wearing lately, and pretended to be all absorbed in my magazine. I ignored Don when he came into the bedroom, but I was only half covered so he could tell the thong was on. 'Did Winnie get demoted?' he asked, grinning from ear to ear. At that moment I realized that wearing a Disney character to bed probably wasn't the biggest turnon for my guy!

"Needless to say, we ended up having an incredibly steamy night. When it was all over and Don was snoring, I decided to run out of underwear more often!"

Sparkplugs: The Food of Love

- Kiss the chef: "From the obligatory anniversary dinner to the unexpected glass of fresh-squeezed juice, the act of preparing food for another (or with another) speaks louder and clearer than most words. It says with no exceptions, 'I love you. I want you. I care for you. You are worth the effort.'"[6]

- "Even before we married, my husband and I loved to spend time in the kitchen together, cooking. Since we had Serena, we have tried to keep up with this habit. When she's finally asleep, we'll put on some Andrea Bocelli in the CD player and start chopping, grating, and boiling. I usually make the red sauce, and Doug will put together the salad and the bread. Pretty soon the whole kitchen is filled with yummy smells of tomato and garlic and spices. For us, a perfect pasta meal is incomplete without candles (unscented, so as not to spoil the aroma of the food), a beautiful tablecloth, and conversation. We often toast each other with some kind of sweet—okay, corny—compliment like, 'To Shannon, the sexiest mom in America' or 'To Doug, who always puts me in the mood for *amoré.*'" Then we usually bust out laughing. But we are in a great mood, and that, combined with good talk, good food, and an Italian dessert from the deli, gets us raring to go!" —Shannon

- "On Saturday mornings, my husband lets me sleep in while he gets up with our three kids. This alone is a great big boost to my spirits, and the extra rest gives me the zip

I've been lacking from chasing the kids all week. He'll make pancakes on the griddle, and sometimes as a treat he'll bring up a tray with heart-shaped pancakes and a mug of Starbucks coffee. Of course, this puts me in a really sweet mood, and once in a while, if we time these breakfasts in bed just right, the kids are totally captivated by Saturday morning cartoons and...well, suffice it to say that the best way to a woman's heart is through heart-shaped pancakes and a few extra hours of sleep!" —Charlene

- "Craig and I are total foodies, and we love to try new foods and drinks. For our anniversary, my parents got us a subscription to a coffee-of-the-month club, and we got hooked on getting a gourmet package of coffee in the mail every month. When that expired, we decided to sign up for a cheese-of-the-month club, and now we are working through a chocolate-of-the-month club. It's kind of expensive sometimes, but it gives us both something to look forward to sharing each month. These treats, whatever they are, are off-limits to the kids. We try to keep them just for ourselves. One time we snuck off to our walk-in closet to try the new chocolates, and one thing led to another and we ended up making love on the floor of the closet! Between the risk of getting caught (not very high, but still a little risk) and the chocolates, we were like a couple of teenagers in the backseat of a car." —Liz

- "When you're done eating Chinese takeout, offer to read your husband's fortune cookie for him. No matter what it reads, say, 'You will be very happy and very naked as soon as you clear the table.'"[7]
- "When you send your man to the supermarket, make a few sexy additions to the grocery list: champagne, strawberries, fishnet stockings…anything that'll get his mind racing."[8]

SEVEN

Sure, Your Man Is from Mars...but Aren't Martians Cute?

Beating the Libido Busters, Part 4:
His Needs, Her Needs

T he night of the red and black lingerie was an overwhelming success. The passion Trevor and Debra felt for each other that night was almost what it had been in the early days of their marriage. The next morning—and, indeed, for several days after that— Deb and Trevor felt connected again in a way that had eluded them for far too long. They laughed more and treated each other with more respect and care. Trevor was more attentive to Debra, asking her about her day and pitching in with the housework a bit more. She in turn was kinder, less sarcastic, and more interested in listening to him wax on about his precious Calgary Flames, who were in the play-offs.

Inevitably, real life intervened, and Trevor and Debra lost their tenuous link once again. First Avery got the flu, then Micah, and finally the whole family. Trevor was anxious about the possibility that his job might be outsourced. This made him edgy and hard to be around. Debra was in a blue funk because her beloved grandmother had died. Pretty soon they were once more like two ships passing in the night.

If Trevor ever initiated sex, he usually had pretty bad timing. One morning, after Deb had been up most of the night with a vomiting Micah, Trevor burst into their bedroom with a gleam in his eye. "Hey, babe! Micah's asleep, Avery's at Molly's, and we have a solid half hour at our disposal."

Debra just stared at him. "Are you crazy? I was up all night while you lay there and snored, so you can just forget it!" She rolled over and fumed for the better part of an hour.

Then there was the time she had major PMS, and all she wanted at the end of the day was to run out of the house and be by herself. Micah had been particularly clingy that day. Trevor, not the most intuitive man on the planet, failed to pick up on Deb's body language, which was definitely not saying, "Take me now!" After she got back from the library, where she had spent an hour or so browsing, Deb started to do the supper dishes. Why hadn't Trevor realized that Deb was in no frame of mind to do the dishes? Couldn't he see that they needed to be done? Irked, tense, and already feeling cramps in her abdomen, Deb just wanted to finish the dishes and drop into bed. Trevor picked that moment to come up behind her and grab her breast. "Don't!" she hissed at him through gritted teeth. Then she burst into tears and ran upstairs. Wounded, Trevor threw up his hands in mock despair. "Women!"

Vive la Différence?!

We all know it: you and your husband have completely different notions about sex. And therein lies the rub (or lack of rub). This is a vast generalization, but *typically* men hanker for more time in the bedroom than their womenfolk do. Guys also seem to crave more variety, and their motives for wanting nooky in the first place are different from ours. Of the factors that galvanize them to want sex, says Kevin Leman, "a number of them are emotional and spiritual, having nothing to do with the physical. I'm your average Joe who doesn't have eight buddies to talk about life with. All I've got is my wife. And if she's too busy with the kids and I repeatedly get sent into the dugout, I tell myself: She doesn't care. She doesn't know what I'm up against."[1]

Male and female sexuality is so intrinsically different, it's a wonder we ever come together. Even drug companies are finding *la différence* to be a real drag: some twenty million men all over the globe have turned to Viagra for help in the last several years, and now pharmaceutical giants are in a frenzy trying to formulate a female equal. Of course, their feverish efforts have so far been a waste of time and money because, of course, there are very tricky mental and emotional components that affect a woman's sexual response. Nothing works as well as Cialis and Viagra.

Why? How come few couples have equal amounts of the hots for each other? Here are a few reasons:

Biology, Baby

Testosterone, one of the hormones responsible for sex drive, is 20 to 40 percent more prevalent in men than women. This physiological reality means your guy is probably going to want you 20 to 40 percent more often than you want him. Yes, that's a problem. (My friend Annie went on a low dosage of testosterone to muster up more interest in sex after her son was born. Not only did Annie's sex drive get fired up, for the first time in her life, she started noticing the makes and models of cars! I am not making this up! Fortunately, she didn't experience any weird hair growth, and that's a good thing.)

Also, a woman's sex drive can be quite fragile, while a man's is usually much more durable. Let me explain with this analogy: if a woman's sex drive is a thin cotton, a bit wispy and delicate, a man's drive can be compared to some sort of Teflon-coated canvas material from which army tents are made. If a guy's in the mood, he's in the mood. Neither rain, nor sleet, nor snow, nor hail will interfere with a man's desire to deliver. A woman, on the other hand, may have a perfectly viable impulse to have sex, but then, you know, something will come up, and she'll suddenly realize she's not so inclined to go through with her impulse. Have you ever had the experience of being in the mood and then having the mood mysteriously go *poof* for no good reason? I know I have, and it's no fun explaining to the man of the house that, true, half an hour ago sex sounded fabulous, but now I would really just rather read this juicy novel. Another quandary, my friends.

Emotional Motivations

You've heard the saying, "Men are like microwaves and women are like Crock-Pots." Guys, generally speaking, are ready, willing, and able to get busy between the sheets even if they've just had a blowup with their wives or tension is thick over some issue. (Let's say he didn't feel like holding down the fort while she went to get her hair done.) Girls, we know if we've just had a fight, big or small, and the making up hasn't been adequate, we ain't doing the deed with him no matter how long it's been! Women usually need to feel emotionally close to their lovers to want sex. We simply must be on the same page, feeling like partners in regard to the house and the kids, for us to give of ourselves in a sexual way. A husband will typically operate in reverse manner. Our men need to feel close to us physically before they invest a great deal of emotional energy in their marriages.

Consider Sally Slow Cooker, who is doing the slow burn over some offense caused by her husband. Frankly, she's steamed. She's waiting for the guy in her life to apologize or even make some overture that indicates he's willing to talk about it. She's in absolutely no frame of mind to be seduced, let me tell you! Microwave Mike, however, is feeling frisky and can't quite figure out what's bothering his wife this time. If Sally would be more tuned in to him physically, he reasons, he'd be a whole lot more willing to concede he's been a bit of a jerk. News flash to Mike: bacon will fly before Sally's going to do the futon-fandango with a man she feels emotionally distant from. Clue to Sally: Mike's not going to want to resolve the matter at hand, really, unless he's feeling physically close to you.

And round and round we go, a dilemma with a capital *D*.

Perceived Injustices

Many of us moms who wear numerous hats are irritated—if not downright ticked—that our husbands don't help us out more. Herewith, my friends, we have come upon a hot-button issue to the extreme: division of labor. Kevin Leman, that funny, funny man, once wrote a book called *Sex Begins in the Kitchen: Because Love Is an All-Day Affair.* Embedded in that book title is one big simmering kettle of fish. No matter what, no woman is going to get all hot and bothered over a man whom she feels could—and should be pulling more of his weight around the house. Why? Because resentment is a huge lust buster.

Dr. Pierre Assalian, the chief psychiatrist at Montreal General's department of psychiatry, states what we moms know intuitively: "An exhausted woman won't be a [sexually] responsive one. A new mother who washes dishes and laundry, and puts the kids to bed every night probably won't often be in the mood. Her partner has to pitch in."[2]

In Christian circles we talk a lot about mutual submission and serving our spouses in love. Of course this is the goal, something wonderful and good to work toward with the powerful help of the Holy Spirit. But, being human, we are known for falling short. Sometimes our efforts break down, and there is a glaring inequity in who does what around the house.

Basically, it boils down to this: a woman will be much more receptive to lovemaking if she feels cared for and supported. Research shows that women end up resentful or dissatisfied with the relationship when they do more work than their partners. If her husband comes home from work after she's had a frazzling day with the kids and plops down to watch the game without seeming to give a fig about her, chances are excellent he'll get a frosty glare in response to his come-hither look.

Consider this scenario: A friend of mine has a husband who has refused for a number of years to buy a dishwasher for their home. He is just a practical guy who thinks it's a waste of money. Hey, no one's arms are broken in their house! They could probably afford a dishwasher, although money is usually somewhat tight. But she works part time and has offered to pay for the appliance out of her income. Well, you know how that goes. Her money is his money and his money is her money. But he's still the guy paying the bills and balancing the checkbook. And he's digging in his heels: no dishwasher even if it would save them both time and energy.

You know where I'm going with this little saga. That crazy dishwasher has become like the white elephant in the room that no one talks about. And you know exactly where that white elephant spends quality time: in their bedroom. Alice, my rather miffed buddy, admits she doesn't often feel turned on by a man who, out of thrift and stubbornness, won't budge and fork over a reasonable amount of money for an appliance that most of the modern world enjoys on a daily basis. She's tired and aggravated, and as a result, Cheapo Charlie doesn't get his motor tuned up too often. Obviously, the issue here isn't really about the dishwasher; it's about Alice feeling unsupported and uncared for.

For many of you, division of labor isn't a matter of contention. You've found a way to balance the extra work of child rearing, shifting chores here and there to accommodate your own personal energy levels and job status, and you're both okay with that.

But for the rest of you, this is one huge enchilada of an issue.

Men Think About Sex More Than We Do

Ya think? Maybe it's their testosterone, but guys simply cogitate the mysteries of the universe somewhat less often than women and ponder, well, sex. "Supposedly, guys want to have sex about two hundred times a day. Supposedly, we are thinking about it when we wake up, when we eat breakfast, when we drive the car, when we read the paper," says Peter Downey, author of *Dads, Toddlers, and the Chicken Dance.* "Supposedly, we are thinking about it all the time."[3] (I asked my husband about this, and he looked at me in that frightened there-is-no-right-answer-to-this-question way.) How often do we ladies mull over the activity that has our male counterparts so thoroughly absorbed? We ruminate about it when we've had a hot dream, maybe, or if we've read a magazine article entitled "Teach Him These Moves Tonight!" or if we're actually doing it or about to do it, or possibly when our husbands obviously want to do it. Which is to say, less often, to be sure.

Men Have a Different Sense of Timing

Oh, do they really? Yes, dear ladies, it's quite safe to say they do. And it's also quite safe to say that's the understatement of the millennium. Timing is critical to the success of such endeavors, and for whatever reason—call me crazy—the tempo of a man and the cadence of his lover can be off. Sometimes way off, if the response of my Dish friends is any indication, but we'll get to them in a moment. What could be the merging of two swelling movements in a beautiful crescendo is often ruined because the third-chair tuba comes in about six bars too early. I think you know what I'm talking about. Peter Downey does: "My guess is most of us [men] have a poor awareness when it comes to picking appropriate moments to pursue sex," he writes. "It's almost as if our libidos are out of chronological sync with our wives. We pick the worst time of the day and, therefore, we often face rejection."[4]

When we reject our husband's advances just because the timing isn't right, he is likely to take the rejection personally even if we don't intend to send that message. We honestly think we would accept the overtures of our favorite tuba player at a better time.

❀ THE DISH: "CAN'T YOU SEE THIS ISN'T A GOOD TIME?"

Why are our husband's ideas about timing and sex so vastly different from ours? That's one of the mysteries of the universe, like Stonehenge, only more baffling. Maybe women's relative lack of enthusiasm is one of those inborn birth-control methods our Creator gave us so we wouldn't have twelve children apiece. I just dunno. One thing I do know is that my panel of pals gave quite a shout out about this topic. Guys are famous for bad timing, it seems, because they have, well, bad timing:

"One time my husband wanted to do this thing with sherbet—you know what I mean." My friend, let's call her "Anabelle," rolled her eyes. "I had been cleaning up vomit all day because our toddler had the stomach flu. I think because of the day I'd had and the state of mind I was in, creative experiments in bed were the last thing I wanted to do. I burst into tears and said, 'I've been cleaning up messes all day, and the last thing I want to do is clean up one more mess!'"

Joy chimed in: "Usually when I am scrambling around, getting ready to have people over for care group meeting or whatever, Chad will come up behind me and be all frisky," she says. "I'm like,

'Can't you see I'm running around trying to get the house ready and this isn't a good time?'"

A couple of ladies complained that their guys seemed oblivious to their energy levels. Fatigue is a big deterrent to passion as it is. But when she's too tired to paint her nails and he's wanting to break out the chocolate body paint, the man's going to run into a brick wall. "Just after dinner Steve said he couldn't wait for later," says Amy, "but by the time we got the kids into bed and then got ready ourselves, I could not muster enough energy even to kiss passionately, let alone do anything else!"

Erika cracked me up when she talked about her husband's off-kilter advances: "He'll want to have sex late, when I'm all cozy and warm and under the covers for the night," she says. "I mean, I've usually got my hot-water bottle clamped between my feet by then!" What's a little hot-water bottle between lovers? Actually, it's a big fat clue that Erika would rather do just about anything than disturb her comfy reverie. That hot-water bottle may as well be a hot-water tank for the obstacle it presents to her husband.

Let me offer another hint that now is not a good time for a roll in the hay: when it's obvious that the lady of the house is trying to escape for a while, even if that escape is within the four walls of the house. "I love to take showers—burning hot," says Marisol. "It's my time to get away. When one of my kids was a baby, I was having this blissful, wonderful hot shower, and suddenly John opened the curtain and came in there with me. I gave him a glare, actually.

I thought he wouldn't notice, but he did! He didn't know what he had done wrong. At that moment, though, I couldn't give anything to one more person."

Okay, let's catalog the results of our little survey: It's a bad time for making love, boys, when we are exhausted, need to flee the domestic grind, feel overworked, or are strung out because we've cleaned up one too many messes for the day. And a hot-water bottle between our feet is a clear keep-out sign if ever there was one. But when is a good time? The girls weigh in:

Pillow Talk

Instead of Saying This...	Say This...
"When you're done, can you run out to the store and pick up some milk?"	"Next time we try that, let's add some whipped cream! Which reminds me, let's put that on the grocery list. Oh, and while you're at it, a gallon of milk, too."
"Shh...they are just about to do the reveal on *Trading Spaces*."	"Boy, that was definitely worth turning off the tube for!"
"I've been going over our 401(k) statements and..."	"I've been going over some magazine articles, and there's something I want to try with you. Lie still, stud muffin!"
"Zzzzzzzzzzz..."	"Well, well, well! We should go to bed early more often!"
"My leg goes where?"	"Hmm...this is fascinating, but let me try moving the other way, and let's see what happens!"

"The worst time to suggest sex to me is anytime I'm feeling totally overloaded," says Ann. "So good times would be, say, after Dan has offered to make dinner, do the dishes, and put Adam to bed—essentially giving me some time to feel human again. Another good time is after I've had some time out of the house by myself with girlfriends and am feeling generally appreciative of him giving me time to relax."

Lisa concurred that there are some circumstances more favorable than others for passion to unfold. "When the kids are away, the house is together, I'm at that time of the month when I'm not carrying extra water weight, we're not crazy-stressed about money, and we've been nice to each other all day—that's a good time," she says. "Some people are fair-weather skiers. I'm a fair-weather sexy mama."

❀ MOJO MAKEOVER: STRIVE FOR SIMPATICO IN THE SACK

Try these ideas and see if you and your man can't synchronize your urges a little better.

Stop Blaming the Differences

Girls will be girls and boys will be boys, so let's stop expecting our lover to think like a woman! It's crucial for both parties to become more understanding of each other. Imagine what it's like to be him, with that extra 20 to 40 percent of testosterone juice rushing through his veins, not to mention being blitzkrieged by sensual images of half-naked women every time the guy turns around. Consider the fact that your husband is not a clueless jerk so much as he is a guy, subject to random fits of desire for you that may not always fit conveniently into your schedule. Yes, it would help the menfolk to understand that their wife is not necessarily a passionless, frigid being, but a creature who needs an emotional connection before she'll feel like having a sexual connection. Stop blaming each other for being what you intrinsically are: different! Ultimately, the blame—not the differences in libido—is what will shred a relationship.

Investigate New Incentives

By and large, the two sexes don't really understand that each is motivated by different enticements to be intimate. For men, making love is a means to be close to you on a heart-and-soul level. Sex is a vehicle for confirmation that they are loved and wanted. When the urge to merge strikes them, it's not only about physical release; it's also about being close to you. "Women, this might surprise you, but even more than your husband wants to have sex with you for his own sexual relief, the truth is, he wants to please you even more than he wants to be pleasured," says Dr. Leman. "When sex dies in a marriage, a man loses something very important to him—

the knowledge that he can please his wife physically. And a woman loses the satisfaction that she has a man who is enthralled by her beauty."[5] Grasp that, ladies, and you will have learned volumes about the man you married.

Meanwhile, your honey needs to comprehend why and how you become romantically inspired. Guys need to reach out to their sweeties in emotional and affectionate ways in order for them to be seduction-ready. When men and women get why our partner wants sex, we'll be more understanding, more open to making it work.

Divvy Up the Labor

Some of you might think it's manipulative of me to suggest that your husband might get lucky more often if he simply dunked a few forks in soapy water or folded a few loads of Onesies. But it's reality. We gals do feel more loving when we sense that our lovers have our best interests at heart, when we feel that we are true partners.

Do you allow your guy to pitch in and lighten your load? Many women try to be Supermom and then blame hubby when they wear themselves out. Ask for and help organize the support that you need in order to be a happy, effective parent and an amiable wife. Be sure to tell your partner that, the way you and most women are wired, a prerequisite to a hot sex life is you feeling as if you have his support around the house. And do check out *Sex Begins in the Kitchen* by Kevin Leman for more info on division of labor and how it relates to your love life.

In truth, your guy will probably think it's not a bad trade-off at all to bathe the younguns, give you a break, and put you in the mood for a splashy finale later that night. Sex should never be used as a weapon or even a bargaining chip, but sharing the load will grease the wheels of your sexual union, which in turn will help the other components of your life together run more smoothly.

Just Say It

"George is very good at reading my 'open' signals," says Emily. "I've always said it never hurts to ask, even though the answer may not always be yes. I try to read his body language as well and be sensitive to how he's feeling."

Say, out loud mind you, what you feel when he's putting on the pressure and either you're just not in the mood or it's not a good time. Vocalize that you love and adore him and think he's incredibly hot, but that currently you feel a wee bit wrung out on account of the fact that your toddler had a record number of blowouts today, and, gee, would he take a rain check? This, my friends, is a far superior plan to just clamming up and hoping the guy will figure it out with the brains God gave him. (By the way, most men *will* take a rain check!) Maybe talking about it yourself will encourage your partner to open up about how he feels when his overtures are rejected. Getting a constructive dialogue going about why and how badly and how often you want to have sex can be the difference between harmony and strife.

While we're on the subject of talking, be sure to have the all-important good-time/bad-time discussion. "Jason," you might say (if your husband's name is Jason), "I also want us to find more time for unbridled passion. I would say the best times for me are when I feel supported and cared for by you, like the other day when you started dinner and listened to me vent about my mom." Then, when you have Jason's attention, gently outline for him the times when his chances are less favorable. "You know how the baby screamed for three hours from colic and I was crying because I was so stressed out? That wasn't really a good time." When your man has some sort of guidelines to follow, he'll try to follow them, believe me! Always focus on the positive, that you love making love—especially when you've had a good day. Humor is another excellent way to grease the wheels of your discussion. And don't shut him down with an abrupt, negative response to his proposition ("Are you on drugs?"). Finally, give your rain check some credibility by suggesting a specific time: "Baby, I am just so tired from my day. But let's shoot for tomorrow night because I have something new in mind that I've been wanting to try." I think he'll go for it. He'll survive until tomorrow night and be secretly relieved you're not rejecting him and his manliness. He'll also think he has a sweet and sexy wife who is planning on both getting naked with him in less than twenty-four hours and trying out a new move! Who could ask for anything more?

Just Do It

If you wait for the perfect opportunity to be matched with the perfect mood, you'll be howling at a blue moon before anything happens. Sometimes a quickie does the trick in breaking this nasty cycle: "He wants me, but I'm not in the mood, so I feel guilty, which makes me feel even less in the mood…"

You may not necessarily be in the mood, per se, but once you get going, you may find yourself in a different frame of mind. Seriously, new studies show that waiting for the urge to strike may be pointless because once you get going, mood or no mood, the urge often follows happily behind. Yes, the laundry piles are beginning to teeter, and, true, you'd rather find out what happens in your book than have sex, but a fast romp may do wonders for your relationship. Remember, when your husband bathes the kids when he would rather watch the game or looks you in the eye and listens to how your day went when he'd rather collapse in a chair and zone out, he's acting lovingly despite his preference. You can do the same for him. Sometimes putting aside your wishes to accommodate his needs is a really good thing. "I think that trying to be up for things, as a gift to your spouse, doesn't hurt," says Emily. "Sometimes it is easy to get selfish in a relationship and only respond for your own reasons. Doing something solely for someone else's pleasure brings unexpected pleasure for both."

Just doing it, whether or not you feel like it, also saves you from falling into a rut that could get more pronounced with time. Experts say that going too long between romps can cause your hormone levels to change, which means your mood changes as well. So in some ways, passion is a use-it-or-lose-it kind of deal. And it goes the other way: new research shows that making love inspires desire—the more you have, the more you want!

A Note About Scheduling Sex (And Being in the Mood)

Has it come to this? Must we consult our Franklin planners for a romp in the hay? I have always been opposed to the idea of scheduling passion. After all, either you're in the mood or you're not in the mood, right? Well, maybe I was wrong. I'm just saying maybe. There's a new school of thought on the subject of "being in the mood." Michele Weiner-Davis writes:

> Up until now, many experts in the field of human sexuality
> assumed that all people experience sexual desire in a similar
> way. Something (a sensual person, a revealing photo, an

article of clothing, a scent, romantic or seductive words) triggers a sexy thought or fantasy that, in turn, triggers an urge to act—to become sexual with your partner or engage in self-pleasure. Sexual stimulation then leads to arousal. But some experts are beginning to question this one-size-fits-all perspective on sexual desire. In fact, they're noticing that for some people, sexual desire—the urge to become sexual—doesn't precede feeling aroused, it actually follows it. In other words, though you may rarely (or never) find yourself fantasizing about sex or feeling a sexual urge, if you're open to becoming sexual with your spouse, you will often find the sexual stimulation pleasurable and therefore feel the urge or desire to continue.[6]

In other words, sometimes you can fan the flames by just getting started. Once you're into it, you're into it. Interesting, huh? This phenomenon has happened to me. I've been curled up in bed with a good book, wanting nothing more than to find out what happens to the heroine or hero of my book. Then the man of the house will make some sort of overture, and my first thought is, *Um...no.* But about half the time I put the book down and forge ahead, hoping for the best but not expecting much. And usually I am surprised by how good those little "charity" sessions can be—for me!

Which brings us back to the whole notion of planning a sexual encounter. If in fact "the mood" can actually follow foreplay, then it makes sense that "the mood" could be scheduled, right? Why not try putting a date on the calendar? Les and Leslie Parrott are wild for the concept:

> At least once a month, schedule a specific time when the two of you can enjoy a leisurely time of passionate sex. We know this sounds artificial. We can hear you groaning right now. But please do not make the mistake of thinking this advice is for other couples. Every busy couple with a family can benefit from this.... What would be your ideal of how to make this time everything you want it to be? Talk it through.... Go shopping. In the weeks preceding your time together, be on the lookout for lingerie and such that will make this time special. Before we got married, some-one gave me (Les) a copy of Charlie Shedd's book *Letters to Philip,* and in it he suggested a husband should never skimp on the lingerie budget. Pretty good advice, especially for parents. You don't have to break the bank, but for these once-a-month occasions, it's a good idea to splurge a little. Part of what makes this once-a-month experience so bene-ficial to couples is the anticipation of it. Just knowing you will have this dedicated time to enjoy each other to the fullest will make it all the more special. So give in to the

anticipation. Say things to each other like, "Only one more week," and, "I can't wait for the eighteenth," or, "Have you been thinking about our time like I have?" The point is to conjure up expectancy and eagerness. Don't allow your appointment to simply roll around on the calendar like any ordinary meeting. Give it special attention and watch the excitement mount.[7]

That part about watching the excitement mount makes a non-scheduler like myself want to pencil something into my calendar today! Short of actually having a cemented timetable for sex, you could try this compromise: knowing that there are predictable/scheduled times during which passion is a possibility, like naptime or Friday nights, let's say, you could leave the option open. Maybe you'll go for it; maybe you won't. We do a lot of "let's shoot for Saturday night" around here. This makes it kind of spontaneous *and* kind of planned.

Sparkplugs: Bold and Playful Is SO This Year

- Get creative. Sex is not boring! Even lifelong lovers can begin to explore new horizons. Try something fresh. When was the last time you made love out on the deck or checked into a local hotel for a few hours instead of going out to dinner? Try making love with a blindfold on or with your eyes wide open.

- Do we love it or do we *love* it when our husbands surprise us with flowers or some other sweet little surprise? Instead of waiting for him to surprise you, rev up the romance by surprising him—and not only on occasions like Valentine's Day, his birthday, or your anniversary. In lieu of flowers, if he's not a flower kind of guy, try bringing home a banana muffin and some gourmet coffee, a little jug of pure maple syrup and an outdoor magazine, a songbook and some new guitar picks. A good surprise always adds excitement to an otherwise mundane day. He'll love that you were thinking about ways to make him happy.

- Order a set of Get-Lucky Dice from Red Envelope (www.redenvelope.com) and prepare for game time. The four pewter dice feature action words *(caress, kiss)* and body parts *(lips, back)*. Put two and two together, and you'll get more fun than you bargained for!

- Do test-drive the marvelous new K-Y product that "warms on contact." The woman in the television commercial wiggled her eyebrows suggestively when she heard those three words. You will too when you try it!

- Open up a bottle of wine or sparkling grape juice, then slow dance in the living room to some hot jazz.

- Toss a wee slip of lace in your husband's briefcase, backpack, or lunch box—and I don't mean a fabric sample! One woman I know, the wife of a cop, says her husband will periodically find a leopard-print thong or something similar in his briefcase, and he's been nabbed a few times by snickering fellow officers. Far from embarrassing him, the sexy message makes his day. Plus, he's the envy of the precinct.

EIGHT

If You Don't Go Back to Bed Right Now...

Beating the Libido Busters, Part 5:
Kiddus Interruptus

Trevor got something interesting in his Christmas stocking the year Avery turned four and Micah turned one: vouchers for an overnight stay at a bed-and-breakfast. This gift was from his sister Laura and her husband, Duane. They had enjoyed several weekends at the same B&B, which wasn't far from Trevor and Laura's parents' house.

"Um, thanks, guys!" Trevor said, obviously a little bemused by the gift. He shot a look at Deb. "Do they take kids at this place?"

They had yet to leave Avery for even one night despite the fact that she was four.

"No!" His sister squealed delightedly, as if she were giving him the best news of his life. "That's the best part!" Laura and Duane smirked at each other in a way that made everyone else laugh. It didn't take a rocket scientist to figure out what had happened between the two of them at the Willow Branch Inn. Trevor rolled his eyes. "Too much information, Laura." She could be so obvious sometimes. But, also obviously, whatever she and Duane were doing was working. Laura usually sat on Duane's lap for some portion of every family gathering, or they would start making out in the middle of a football game. "Get a room," Trevor would quip on these occasions. Of course his sister and brother-in-law ignored him completely.

Secretly, Trevor was kind of jealous. Laura and Duane weren't perfect—even they had their moments of friction—but at least they were still making out twelve years after they got married, no less. Their kids were seven and five, not much older than his own, a fact Trevor would point out when he suggested to Deb that they leave the kids with his parents for a night. And he didn't say this, but privately he noticed that Laura's kids were much closer to his parents than his were. He knew it was because they had spent a fair amount of time alone with Grandma and Grandpa.

So far Debra wasn't ready to leave the kids overnight. At first it was breast-feeding—she couldn't leave a breast-fed child, now could she? Debra had a point there. But now Micah was one and pretty much weaned. Maybe at this point she would consider it.

Trevor would have been quite surprised to know that Debra was indeed open to getting away. She knew the kids would be fine without her for one night, and the thought of going to that adorable bed-and-breakfast was very appealing. Besides, she and Trevor could use some time together. Without the kids.

After all, on those rare evenings when the planets aligned and both Debra and Trevor were reasonably up for romance, Avery would inevitably barge into their bedroom. If they made her go back to bed, she would scream her head off for the better part of half an hour, shattering their amorous mood. Trevor thought Deb wasn't strict enough with Avery when it came to bedtimes. "I sure never got up five times after my parents put me to bed," he said in disgust. "Who runs this show anyway? Our kid or us?"

Debra knew Trevor was right, but she felt defensive about her mothering skills. Why *wasn't* Avery more obedient when it came to bedtime? Deb wanted just one evening when she could go to bed early and read peacefully for an hour before she drifted off. Was that too much to ask? In their house it apparently was.

One night Avery went down quite easily, and both Debra and Trevor were up for some action. They dispatched with any preamble and got down to business right away. Why waste a golden opportunity? Just as they were getting to the good part, though, they heard their door squeak. Deb's heart sank. Trevor groaned in frustration. "Mommy?" a little voice said in a high-pitched whisper. "I'm tirsty, Mommy."

Both of them sighed. It was all over. They knew that much. By the time Debra got Avery settled (she already had water in her bedroom), Trevor was sawing logs.

❧ HOW LONG HAVE YOU BEEN STANDING THERE?

Kiddus interruptus, says Peter Downey, is that oh-so-mood-busting moment when, in the throes of passion, you notice your child has materialized in the room with you and is staring at you quizzically. "Obstacles to a great sex life?" quips Mary. "How about deciding on the living room for romance and opening my eyes to see our three-year-old watching quietly from the doorway of her bedroom?" That'll stick a fork in libido every time—for Mary and the rest of us.

Who hasn't had an inopportune visit from one of their kids just as things were heating up in the bedroom? Depending on the age of your child, the event may not be all that terrible—for the child, that is. For you, though, an interruption always causes embarrassment, horror, and the fear that your kid will someday have a therapy bill greater than his college loans.

I must pause to share with you the oft-told tale of my husband and his two sisters, who once caught Ma and Pa *in flagrante delicto.* Lorraine, Doyle's oldest sister, saw through a crack in her parents' bedroom door an unmistakable vision of her folks knowing each other in a biblical way. Of course she summoned her siblings. The three of them stacked up like cordwood by the door, peeking and sniggering until the folks noted six wide eyeballs peeping at them. That was the end of that show, but not of the account, which has grown into a big fat joke over the years. By the way, none of the three kids was unduly scarred by this incident, which has been comforting to me in my own throes of *kiddus interruptus.* (See "Tales from the Love Shack" later in this chapter.)

Why do we come unglued at the thought of our offspring witnessing our intimate moments? After all, pioneers in sod houses were compelled to conduct their sex lives just a few feet away from their tykes. This boggles my mind! Many people I know can't even concentrate on sex when their little babies are sleeping in a bassinet next to the bed, never mind if their six children were five feet away and possibly awake. And those lovers of yore didn't even have the luxury of fans to provide white noise! I don't know how our forebears ever passed their seed on to subsequent generations, but I do know that most of us modern parents are flipped into next week when our cherubs halt our most private reverie with a surprise appearance.

"I don't think we will ever forget when my son was about three," says one flabbergasted mom. "We didn't shut the door and were so involved we didn't hear him come in. Next thing you know, my husband gets hit on the bottom with a plastic baseball bat! Really ruined the moment to say the least."[1]

It's not only disconcerting to worry about what effect the surprise had on the kid, but it also spoils the mood for Mom and Dad in a big way. Nothing says "arrrrgh!" like a thwarted orgasm. Between fatigue, bad timing, body image, and any other number of sexual stressors, it's hard enough to get revved up for a parley of pleasure without having to worry about a munchkin break-in.

❀ THE DISH: SOUNDPROOF WALLS? YEAH RIGHT

The following two divulgences will make you giggle and probably prompt you to say, "Been there, done that" or "I feel your pain, sister." Incidentally, though these things are never any fun whatsoever when they are happening, time and space and a new lock on the door can turn episodes of *kiddus interruptus* into great stories—maybe not to share with the grandkids, but at least with commiserating peers.

Tera dished about the time her night of whooping it up came to a grinding halt: "We recently moved into a new house, one the builder told us—with a wink-wink—came with soundproof walls in the master bedroom. Well, one night my husband and I were getting into it, and I was becoming more and more vocal. My inhibitions were gone, mostly because I had the security of knowing that no sounds would get past those walls to our five-year-old son's room down the hall. Suddenly there was a knock at the door: 'Mommy! Be quiet!' my son said through the door. 'You're being so loud I can't even sleep.' Of course I froze, paralyzed by the thought that my son was scarred for life. But even after he went back to bed and we could have resumed things (in more hushed tones, of course), I just didn't feel the same way." Nothing like throwing a wet blanket on the flames of passion.

Then there's Cherine, whose saga of climbing the mountain of love and being robbed of that great peak experience will ring true with most of us. "Did I tell you about Ava's big fit the other night? Brian and I were getting hot and heavy, and things were about to get really great. Then Ava, who had just turned three, started wailing. We thought she had been asleep for some time, but no. She was wailing. Brian, who never, ever swears, actually did swear then. I could hardly blame him as I felt like swearing myself. We never did figure out what was wrong with Ava, but she insisted on staying in our bed for an hour. Any passion we felt was over by then, trust me."

Debra Sticks to Her Guns

Deb knew something had to be done to curtail Avery's nighttime routine. The next morning she went on the Internet to her favorite parenting Web site and typed in *bedtime hassles* in the search box. Up came a dozen or so articles by parenting experts on how to make a preschooler stay in bed. Finally Deb came upon a concept that intrigued her because it seemed as if it might actually work with her daughter.

That night, when Avery came out of her bed first wanting water and then saying she was scared of monsters, Deb sat down with her. "Avery, sweetie, you have to start staying in bed after we tuck you in," she said. "You have a big night-light in here, and Daddy chased away all the monsters with monster spray. You have a cup full of water right beside your bed. There's no reason to get up. So if you get up again tonight, I will have to take away your Polly Pockets for tomorrow."

Larder for the Libido

In their book *Intercourses: An Aphrodisiac Cookbook*, Martha Hopkins and Randall Lockridge whip up a bevy of artisanal dishes, one and all concocted with supposedly aphrodisiac foods. The recipes are gorgeous, but what's really intriguing are the stories of how and why these foods came to signify sexual love. Here's a sampling:

- Asparagus: Phallic? Yes, but there's more. According to Hopkins and Lockridge, the green veggie also offers lovers a "natural dose of the 'sex vitamin' necessary for increased hormone production."[2]

- Chocolate: Montezuma drank gallons of the stuff to boost his potency. Plus it's infused with the same substance (phenylethylamine) that "courses through the veins of one who is in love."[3]

Avery's eyes began to water. "But Mommy...I wuv my Powwy Pockets! I want dem!"

"I know, Ave, but Mommy needs you to stay in bed. You can keep your Polly Pockets and play with them all day if you stay in bed. But if you come out of bed, I'll have to take them away."

Half an hour later, Avery crept out of bed. "Mommy, I have to go potty, and I can't get my 'jamas wifted up." That was a new one. Debra sighed. Obviously Avery was going to test her on this thing.

- Oysters: Ah, yes, that ageless symbol of eroticism, the lusty oyster looks kind of naughty and is also packed with zinc, which powers the production of testosterone.

- Honey: The birds and the bees. Springtime. Nectar. Need we say more about honey? Okay, we will. It's sweet, sticky, and sensuous as an afternoon in the tent with Solomon and Shulamith, who, by the way, would recommend honey by way of example.

- Strawberries: Dipped in chocolate or consumed naked and ripe, the strawberry "fits easily betwixt parted lips."[4]

- Also reported to be foods of amoré: bananas, caviar, celery, champagne, fennel, garlic, ginger, nutmeg, peppers, radishes, truffles, and vanilla.

"Okay, Ave," she calmly. "If it's easier, take off your pajamas and then go to the potty. And, sweetie, remember what I said about getting out of bed? Tomorrow you may not play with your Polly Pockets."

Avery screamed for thirty minutes, then finally fell asleep in a huff. The next morning was difficult. Debra was tired, and she felt worn down by Avery's whining about the Polly Pockets. It was a long day, but Deb held her ground. That night she repeated her speech about not getting up. This time, Avery stayed in bed.

Trevor was impressed. "Way to go, Deb!" he said. They might have celebrated by making love, but Debra was too exhausted from Avery's whining and complaining. But they did talk for a while that night, planning their family vacation to the beach and joking about sharing a condo with Laura and Duane. "I hope the walls aren't too thin," Deb teased, "'cause she's your sister and all." Trevor rolled his eyes. "Yeah, those two are something else. I'm going to specifically ask for thick walls. Very thick walls!"

✿ MOJO MAKEOVER: SING THE PRAISE OF DEADBOLTS

If this book can at all help you regain a marvelous marriage filled with passion and romance, the youngsters have simply got to stay out of your room—or anywhere else you fancy having a fling. "Leave your mother persona at the bedroom door to rescue your sexual self," says Valerie Davis Raskin.[5] That's an excellent idea, but in order for Mother Persona to be left at the door, Kiddie Persona must have no chance to enter it. There's just no good way to abandon yourself to passion when you're even mildly concerned about one of the kids busting in. You can tweak every single other aspect of your sex life, but if you don't have privacy, you got *nada*.

Here are some strategies to safeguard your inhibitions, ensure the secrecy of your sensual life, and allow you the freedom to play with a carefree disregard of your progeny.

Believe It: They'll Survive

The kids will be fine while you and your hubby do the horizontal bop. (Thank you, ZZ Top, for that fine euphemism!) The bleach is hidden in a locked cabinet, any choking hazards have been confiscated, and the gate is up on the top of the stairs so Turbo Tot, clad in flame-retardant pajamas, can't fall down. He's been bathed, read to, snuggled, prayed with, and tucked in with a capital T. The rascal even has a sippy cup of water, should his thirst need quenching between now and breakfast. There's no earthly reason why he should need you in the next hour or so.

Even so, most of us, being the doting materfamilias that we are, still feel as if we're on call. We can't quite get it out of our head that our child might need us, which is actually a bunch of baloney. He doesn't need you. You've catered to his every whim for the past twelve hours, and now it's your turn. True, kids have their wily ways of infiltrating their parents' time together, but the vast majority of the time they will be perfectly fine without you. I know, I know. Kids puke, they have nightmares, they are scared of the bogeyman. But you should know by now that if you let them, children will take and take and take until there's nothing left for you to give them. Sex is important, as we've established. Go have some, for goodness' sake, and don't worry about the little ones for an hour! As Dr. Phil said to his boys when they were little, "Don't come in this room unless you're on fire!" Once in a blue moon, something will arise which requires your immediate attention. My all-time favorite lust buster? "Mommy, I pooped!" But 90 percent of the time the children will survive quite nicely while their parents attend to their marriage.

Nip Bedtime Hassles in the Bud

Like Avery, most children don't get that Mom and Dad need time alone. Even when told that, no, they can't have another song, story, or back rub at bedtime because it's time for their parents to spend time together, they will fight you with every fiber of their flinty wills. Specifically, many young parents struggle on a nightly basis with long-drawn-out bedtime routines.

Sarah and Mike complained that they were too wiped out for sex after the nightly bathing, tooth brushing, cuddling, and "I'm scared of my closet" ritual. "Somehow, with Caden, one story turns into three or four, and we can never find his stuffed bunny," Sarah says. "I work all day, so I feel guilty when Caden cries that he needs me to sing to him or whatever. Putting him to bed takes two hours, and by then we just drop into our own bed."

Quotable

"Having toddlers is like living with the sex police—they're worse than my parents. Jessica has a sixth sense, crying the moment the bedroom candle is lit. And Isabelle recently found my diaphragm. I said it was a sink plug, to be used only by Mommy for really big leaks. This seemed to satisfy her. But I'll probably find it in the sink next."

—Jennifer Bingham Hull[6]

Again, keep focused on the fact that time together, which may or may not lead to sex, should be a priority. And, like the Beastie Boys said, you gotta fight for your right to party! A thirty- to forty-five minute routine of picking out pj's, brushing teeth, reading one or two stories, praying, and tucking in should be ample. Get a huge night-light if "monsters" are an issue—little ones often have legitimate fears about such things—and leave the door open if that provides comfort. Fill a clean spray bottle with water and spritz "monster spray" under the bed and into the closet. But don't cave on extra cups of water or unnecessary trips outside the kid's room. If you're consistent every night, not just when you are craving a little hanky-panky, you can establish good boundaries.

Even if the Kids Are Asleep, Lock the Door

Seriously, do it. That way you'll know beyond a shadow of a doubt that you will have no surprise guests. One couple I know had a lock installed on their door, and they will testify it was well worth the cost and effort.

Put White Noise to Work for You

I don't think Doyle and I would have much sex at all—or very, very quiet sex, if any—had we not put a box fan in our room to block out noise. If you're lying there, half interested in what's going on in your bed, yet you have one ear out for the kids, you'll never be able to immerse yourself in lovemaking. And remember poor Tera if you think your walls are soundproof. (It never hurts to test that out.) Fans are good. So are white-noise machines and, sometimes, CD players.

Hide Your Stash

Don't want to explain a Polaroid of yourself in the buff? Me neither. For those and other things related to your ongoing mojo makeover, create an off-limits drawer, box, or basket for lovemaking accessories that you want to keep private—and keep it in a place where your kids won't find it. Maybe a file cabinet would work, or a locked drawer, or a Rubbermaid container that can be safely stored high in the closet. One couple kept lotions, clippings from magazines with ideas, and condoms in the husband's fishing-tackle box. (He had another tackle box for actual tackle.) We have a little book full of notions and positions—with the positions pictured—that once wound up in the wrong little hands. We had some "splainin" to do that day! Don't let it happen to you.

TALES FROM THE LOVE SHACK: OF ROMPS AND RODENTS

It was one of those classic Sunday-afternoon scenarios: the baby was napping, and the four-year-old was having what is loosely termed as "quiet time" at our house.

My husband gave me a lewd look ("lewd" also being loosely termed, but you get the visual). I responded in like wanton manner, and the meaning was quite clear: "Let's make hay while the sun shines." And between you and me, the sun was shining and the hay needed making.

We crept up the stairs, conspiratorial grins on our faces, a child-friendly excuse at the ready—"Mommy and Daddy need a quiet time today too"—and a spring in our steps.

Soon enough, things were percolating, if you catch my meaning.

While during the week we may have been too tuckered out or busy cutting little people's meat or what have you, Sunday had arrived and, with it, an opportunity too good to throw away. Life was pleasant, indeed.

Then we heard it, the unmistakable sound of a child crying. Our child, as it happens. "Mommmmmeeeeee!" *Sob.* "Dadddeeeeee…"

Motion ceased in the room.

"Is he crying?" I asked rhetorically.

"No," my husband said quickly. "He's laughing. That's a happy sound."

"Mommeee…" The voice was coming closer. There was a speedy and efficient rearranging of bedclothes, limbs, and whatnot. Within seconds, the tableau in that bedroom was presentable for all manner of guests—visiting dignitaries, grandparents, and four-year-olds alike.

"Honey, what's wrong?" I asked, when a sad little face popped around the door.

"My gerbil's deeeeaadddd," my son wailed.

His father, still holding on to a shred of hope, tried to put out the fire without actually exiting the bed. "He's not dead! I just saw him, like, what? Twenty minutes ago, running on his wheel! He's very, very healthy, buddy. He's definitely not dead!"

"But he wooks dead, Daddy! Come seeeee!"

"Son, Mommy and Daddy really need this quiet time now, okay? So you just believe Daddy that the gerbil is not dead, and Daddy will come see the gerbil in a few minutes."

Sniveling still, our somewhat mollified youngster shuffled back to his bedroom, no doubt to peer sadly and dubiously at his stationary pet.

"Can gerbils slip into comas?" I wondered, feeling a bit guilty for not tending to my son's crisis.

"Um, I dunno," my mate answered absent-mindedly, already resuming our previous activity. I must admit, my interest in said activity had diminished exponentially with every minute my child was standing next to the marriage bed, howling his head off. *But hey,* I figured, *what is worse, engaging in the pastime at hand, even though I wasn't so gung-ho anymore, or planning funeral arrangements for a rodent?*

It was a tossup, mind you, but opportunities being scarce for such endeavors, I decided to try to get into it again. My dear spouse, of course, had forgotten all about the interruption, the existence of the pet gerbil, and, let's face it, the fact that we had children in the first place.

That's why women get pregnant—because men have such short memories.

I'd like to report that we seamlessly reconvened the act, that our afternoon interlude was a memory-making experience of the kind from which bodice rippers find their inspiration. I'd like to report that, but I can't.

In the interests of effective parenting—and the specter of our son being scarred for life by the sight of his lifeless animal—we threw in the towel. Our bed was not to be the sight of any grand passion that afternoon. Laundry folding, but no passion.

We trooped down the hall to our child's room and discovered that "Gerbie" was in the beginning stages of rigor mortis. By the time the creature had been given a proper burial and our son comforted, the mood was flatter than an Amish egg noodle.

"If Sunday afternoon, with both kids supposedly contained in their rooms, is not a good time for sex, when is a good time?" my husband grumped.

"There is *no* good time," I grumped. "We should just give it up forever and sleep in twin beds like your uncle from Poland, what's-his-name, and his wife, Paprika."

"Hey, Uncle Slaw had about eight kids, remember," he replied, slightly alarmed by my tone. "And it's Aunt Patrika."

We decided to lay full blame for the incident on the gerbil and vowed never to host another rodent in our home—at least as long as we still had a cell of desire flickering in our beings.

"Mommy, can we get another gerbil, *pwease?*" My little one's eyes were pooling with tears, his lower lip jutted out. My resolve melted.

Well, maybe one more gerbil. As long as it is an extremely healthy one.

Sparkplugs: Fantasies and Secrets (and Secret Fantasies) Are Sexy!

• Experts say secrets are powerful. One study reported by a television news magazine monitored the physiological responses of two groups, one that was playing footsie under the table secretly and one that was playing footsie out in the open. The secret group, which had something to hide, had higher heart rates, they were sweating, and some were downright turned on. The other group, whom everyone knew was rubbing the feet of the people across the table, registered *nada* in terms of bodily response. So think about adding an element of secrecy to your close encounters. Here's how Tera created a hush-hush scenario in which she had to keep her covert meeting with hubby off the radar screen: "We were at my in-laws' house one weekend. They have quite a large bathroom, so I was putting on my makeup while my husband was in the shower. After he got out of the shower, he was a little turned on by my being in there. As it happens, I am in the bathroom while he gets ready every day, but this one was different. It was sneaky. It was clandestine. It was at his parents' house—in the bathroom! Good thing they have carpet on the floor!"

- "Share a bedtime story. And I'm not talking about *Green Eggs and Ham!* Read aloud to each other, or pick out your favorite juicy part and read solo. Maybe you'll be inspired to create your own bedtime stories."[7]

- Do you have a fantasy of what you would do with your husband if you could? Have you always wanted to make love in an airplane, in an Oriental carpet store (after hours!), in an elevator? Write down your wish list and share them with your partner. He may not be able to make your dreams come true exactly, but he'll have fun trying. You might even try to do your own at-home version of your fantasy. If you daydream about nooky on the beach, for example, you could recreate a beach scene in your bedroom, with beach towels, fruity drinks, and a CD of ocean waves playing the background.

- "We [men] are lulled into a false sense of security by those incredible articles in women's magazines that abound in grocery stores: 'Ten Steps to a Better Orgasm,' 'How to Please Your Man,' 'You Can Be a Better Lover,' 'Your G Spot: Where It Is and What to Do with It,'" writes Peter Downey. "Reading those titles makes us happy because we think our wives are studying those magazines and that when we get home we will enjoy the fruits of their research."[8] Downey goes on to say that sadly, this is not the case. Women don't actually read those articles, never mind follow through on the tips. Oh, really? Prove him wrong! Lull your man into thinking he might be the beneficiary of those racy magazine headlines—and follow through! Leave one such periodical lying around (but only if your kids are pre-readers)! Dog-ear the pages of the racy article. Read it in front of him. Snicker and make lots of intriguing noises, like *mmm* and *wow!* Finally, lead your guinea pig to the "lab" and let the experimentation begin.

- "My husband and I get a baby-sitter and plan a date—but not a typical, married-couple kind of date. He goes somewhere else to get ready, we meet at an agreed-upon place, and we act as if we've just met. Sometimes we pretend to be someone else. Last time I was a doctor and he was a policeman." —Anonymous

NINE

We Should Do This More Often!

A couple of weeks later Trevor realized that his bed-and-breakfast voucher was about to expire. He thought he might have to twist Deb's arm to get her to go, but actually she readily agreed. The new bedtime regime with Avery was going pretty smoothly, but there were still a few bugs to work out. That girl had more excuses than a crooked politician! And Micah had started waking up, crying, just about the time his parents were crawling between the covers. A night away sounded heavenly.

On the day of the overnight, Deb waffled a little bit. Would Trevor's parents respond to Micah's cries? They were kind of old school, which worried Deb. Would they make her baby "cry it out"? But the pull of Victorian décor and gourmet scones was too strong. She was going!

When it came time to pack her pajamas, Deb had a thought: Why not pull out the red and black ensemble? First she had to find it, though. She hadn't used it for a while. After digging around, Deb finally found the teddy crumpled at the back of her summer-clothes drawer. She decided to pack it—in Trevor's overnight bag. Deb smiled when she pictured his reaction.

❧ A SENSUAL REVIEW

Here we are, at the final chapter of this book. It's my fervent hope that you know much more now about getting in touch with your inner Red-Hot Mama than you did when you picked up this little volume. I'm also hoping that, armed with the info and stories in these pages, you've rolled up your sleeves, ladies, and stoked the home fires again. As we've established, sparking passion doesn't even have to be as hard as rubbing two sticks together—although a little well-placed friction can be lots of fun!

This seems like a great time to review both the virtues of reclaiming *amoré* in your marriage and the big hurdles that stand in our way. (By the way, there's no pop quiz!)

Don't Put Your Kids Ahead of Your Husband

Like Debra, our oh-so-like-us-it's-scary heroine, it's tempting to shove the man in our life to the back burner, where he often sits, simmering, for years and even decades. Laundry needs doing, dishes need washing, homework needs supervising, tiny teeth need brushing—it's not rocket science to see how the glow of romance can get blotted out by all the mundane jobs and day-to-day chores that keep the family machine running. That's why we have to put first things first and make couplehood a priority over parenthood.

Carve Out Time to Be Alone Together

Don't let your marriage evolve into one like Trevor and Debra's. These two became like roommates who happened to have the same kids. After putting each other last for so long, those former lovebirds simply had little to do with each other. They resigned themselves to the distance and from time to time experienced bouts of resentment. Leading parallel but separate lives, they started to fall out of love with each other. Distance in a relationship is love's silent killer! Instead of growing apart from your husband, put a new premium on getting out of the house together for lunch, an evening, an overnight, and maybe even more.

Michele Weiner-Davis has devoted years of counseling and writing to helping hitched people stay hitched. Among her resources is her Web site, www.divorcebusting.com, where she writes that you don't have to rent a hot-air balloon or charter a gondola in Venice to start heating things up between you and your spouse.

Even if it feels weird to spend time together at first, when you two invest energy and time to your love life, both of you and your kids will reap the rewards. When you switch the focus of your attention to your man, and he to you, both of you will begin to feel more cared for, more wanted. "Time together gives people opportunities to collect new memories, do activities they enjoy, laugh at each other's jokes, renew their love," says Michele Weiner-Davis.[1] She also affirms that you don't have to spend a solid month together to spark feelings of warmth and affinity (so that's what they're calling it these days…). Short but consistent times together can do the job just as well, especially if you plan for them and stick to them.

Baby, Baby

Whether you've recently had your first child or your fourth, you know how pregnancy, childbirth, and all the resulting physical and emotional ramifications can throw your romantic life for a loop. By being attuned to the factors at work in your body and soul—physical discomfort, hormones, breast-feeding, hormones, PPD, hormones, fatigue…did I mention hormones?—you can tackle or at least manage them one by one. Then you're off to the races again!

Censor Cultural Messages

Think of it this way: we're the water; cultural messages the tea bag. Even if we're hot, lukewarm, or coldly indifferent (we think) to the never-ending exposure to the media and postmodern values, our views are tinted by them. Only you can flush out those messages and decide for yourself not to be unduly influenced by our culture's view of moms and sexuality.

Learn to Love Your Body and Dress Your Age

Body acceptance is a tricky process—and not a quick one at that. It also requires prayer, inviting the One who made your body to reshape your image of it. Take small steps toward eating healthier, moving your bod, and retraining your mind to think good thoughts about your physique. When these components start to come together, you'll be amazed at the burden (negative body image) that's lifted off your shoulders. Now that you've started noticing how what you wear affects your sense of sensuality, I'm hopeful that you've begun to weed out the granny panties and Eeyore sweatshirts in favor of intimate apparel that reflects your budding Red-Hot Mama, not your fourth-grade teacher, Mrs. Finklebeans.

Celebrate Your Martian's...uh...Uniqueness

Uh-huh. Nothing throws a damper on a potentially steamy evening like the whole man/woman gender gap. But when you start seeing the whole realm of passion, romance, and the act through his glare-free fishing binoculars, you'll become far more understanding of his m.o. The cool thing is that understanding is contagious, and he'll start meeting you halfway. What you do when you're ameetin' is totally up to you! (See those Sparkplugs for some great ideas—and don't say I didn't warn you.)

Take Back the Night

Oh yeah! Little Norman may be the apple of your eye, but he has no business crashing the love shack. Surround your sex life with loving limits for the kids, and the whole family will benefit.

✿ Is It Hot in Here Or...

Once you've decided that you want to make your love life a priority again, all it takes is a little creativity, a flair for flirting, a dash of daring, and your poor man won't know what hit him.

Now that we've affirmed all the reasons why revving up your love life is a stupendous thing for all involved, it's time to put down this book, girlfriend, and hop into horizontal bopping action! But, first, let's find out how Trevor and Debra finally got their groove back...

That night Trevor and Deb were sitting by the crackling fire in the parlor of the B&B. Their hosts had bid them good-night and left them with some cookies and milk. Both were reading magazines and nibbling on the delectable treats.

"I wonder how the kids are doing," Trevor said, leaning over Deb to get another cookie.

"What kids?" Deb said. Trevor chuckled. He was surprised that Deb—of all people—would make a joke like that. But he had to give her credit: The hand-off of the kids had been very smooth. Debra hadn't even seemed upset.

"Hey, Trev, could you do me a favor and run upstairs and find my...my...um...slippers? I stuck them in your bag," Debra said. "There was no room in mine," she added hastily.

Trevor disentangled himself from Debra and the couch. "Okay," he said agreeably. "Are your feet cold or something?"

"Something," she said, smirking.

Two minutes later Trevor was back, grinning from ear to ear. "Oh, I found your 'slippers' all right, missy."

"Oh, you did?"

"Yes, I did!"

"Well, why didn't you bring them down? My feet are cold. In fact, other parts of me are cold too."

Trevor couldn't believe how flirty his wife was being. He loved it! He extended a hand to Deb and pulled her up off the couch. "Let's go warm you up," he said, tugging her toward the stairs.

About an hour later, Trevor and Debra were lying in each other's arms, drowsy and content. The red and black item was dangling from a candle sconce across the room. "Hey, boo," he said softly. "I know I don't say it enough, but I love you." Debra snuggled closer to Trevor. "I love you too, hunkybuns," she said sleepily.

"You haven't called me that cheesy name in eons," he noted, kissing her on the forehead. "Boo?"

"Yeah?"

"We should do this more often."

"We definitely should."

Sparkplugs:
A Potpourri of Pleasure

- Buy some scented massage oil and explore the pleasures of the senses. Touch can be a powerful turnon. When you touch someone in a loving way, any number of hormones flow, including oxytocin and endorphins. And when those hormones get going, the person being touched is going to want more.

- "We like to go to bed a little early and give each other mini massages. These take only a few minutes, help us relax, and aren't nearly as much work as a full-body massage. We try to vary the areas we massage, and all body parts are fair game! These mini massages are good for laughs or further intimacy." —Tanya

- Show and tell. "It can be an incredible turnon for a man to be with a woman who knows just what pleases her—

and isn't shy about showing him! If you aren't being touched in a way that pleases you, take his hand and show him how you want to be touched. Or, touch yourself. Men are visual creatures, and as they say, 'a picture is worth a thousand words.'"[2]

- Invite your husband to teach you something new. "Remember when you were first dating and how your heart would race when he'd teach you to play a G-chord or line up a pool shot? Isn't it time you let your guy feel like hot stuff again? Here's why this move is worth being resurrected: It lets him be both superstar and teacher. Men fall in love for how we make them feel about themselves. The goal is to keep making your man feel that way."[3]

- "After our second baby was born, I bought a journal shaped like a heart, wrote a love letter to my husband on the first page, and then slipped it into his bedside drawer. When he found it, he replied with a poem on the next page and slipped it into my drawer. We've continued the tradition ever since. We don't write in the journal every day, but it's always a treat to open my drawer and see it there." —Heather

Notes

Introduction

1. Les and Leslie Parrott, as quoted in David and Jan Stoop, *The Complete Parenting Book* (Grand Rapids: Revell, 2005), 18.
2. Sex After Kids Poll, www.parents.com, 2002.

Chapter 1

1. Susan Hubbard, as quoted in Johnathon Allen, "Passionate Parents: Keeping Love Alive After the Kids Arrive," 2003, http://dadstoday.com/resources/articles/passionate parents.htm.
2. Michele Weiner-Davis, *The Sex-Starved Marriage* (New York: Simon & Schuster, 2003), www.divorcebusting.com.
3. Kevin Leman, *Sheet Music* (Wheaton: Tyndale, 2003), 4.
4. Stephen Madden, "Growing Closer," *Child,* February 2003, 82.
5. Weiner-Davis, *Sex-Starved Marriage,* www.divorce busting.com.

6. Tim Alan Gardner, *Sacred Sex* (Colorado Springs: Water-Brook, 2002), 5.

7. Linda Dillow and Lorraine Pintus, *Intimate Issues* (Colorado Springs: WaterBrook, 1999), 183.

8. Parrotts, as quoted in Stoops, *Complete Parenting,* 18.

Chapter 2

1. Caitlin Flanagan, "The Wifely Duty," *The Atlantic,* January–February 2003, www.theatlantic.com/doc/prem/200301/flanagan.

2. Johnathon Allen, "Passionate Parents," http://dadstoday .com/resources/articles/passionateparents.htm.

3. Weiner-Davis, *Sex-Starved Marriage,* www.divorce busting.com.

4. Carole-Anne Vatcher, "When Parenting Threatens Your Couple Relationship," September 2004, http://www .torontotherapy.ca/index.html?toronto_therapy_articles .html-content.

5. Valerie Davis Raskin, *Great Sex for Moms* (New York: Fireside, 2002), 42.

6. Joan K. Peters, "Showing Our Love," *Child,* February 2003, 84.

7. Claire Maisonneuve, quoted in Georgie Binks, "Keeping Sex Alive After Having Kids," January 2004, www .mochasofa.ca.

Chapter 3

1. Gary Weaver Li, as quoted in Johnathon Allen, "Passionate Parents," http://dadstoday.com/resources/articles/passionate parents.htm.

2. Karen Scalf Linamen, *Pillow Talk: The Intimate Marriage from A to Z* (Grand Rapids: Revell, 1998), 47.

3. Found on www.parentsoup.com, 2003.

4. Found on www.parentsoup.com, 2003.

5. Elizabeth Fishel, "Our Yearly Night Away," *Child*, February 2003, 80.

6. David Mabry, quoted in Johnathon Allen, "Passionate Parents," http://dadstoday.com/resources/articles/passionate parents.htm.

Chapter 4

1. Pierre Assalian in Binks, "Keeping Sex Alive," www .mochasofa.ca.

Chapter 5

1. Flanagan, "Wifely Duty," www.theatlantic.com/doc/prem/ 200301/flanagan.

2. Raskin, *Great Sex,* 88.

3. Raskin, *Great Sex,* 24.

4. Raskin, *Great Sex,* 88.

5. Raskin, *Great Sex,* 89.

Chapter 6

1. Rosemary Basson, quoted in *Ladies' Home Journal,* September 2003.
2. Debra Waterhouse, *Outsmarting the Female Fat Cell After Pregnancy* (New York: Hyperion, 2003), 31.
3. Waterhouse, *Female Fat Cell,* 33.
4. Waterhouse, *Female Fat Cell,* 33.
5. Waterhouse, *Female Fat Cell,* 33.
6. Martha Hopkins and Randall Lockridge, *Intercourses: An Aphrodisiac Cookbook* (Memphis: Terrace, 1997), 5.
7. Dan Bova, "Sex Moves That Rock My World," *Redbook,* December 2003, 104.
8. Bova, "Sex Moves," 104.

Chapter 7

1. Leman, *Sheet Music,* 16.
2. Assalian in Binks, "Keeping Sex Alive," www.mocha sofa.ca.
3. Peter Downey, *Dads, Toddlers, and the Chicken Dance* (Tucson: Fisher, 2000), 194.
4. Downey, *Chicken Dance,* 195.
5. Leman, *Sheet Music,* 11.
6. Weiner-Davis, *Sex-Starved Marriage,* www.divorce busting.com.
7. Parrotts in Stoop, *Complete Parenting,* 22.

Chapter 8

1. "Sex After Kids" www.ivillage.com, June 2000.
2. Hopkins and Lockridge, *Intercourses,* 14.
3. Hopkins and Lockridge, *Intercourses,* 9.
4. Hopkins and Lockridge, *Intercourses,* 47.
5. Raskin, *Great Sex,* back-cover copy.
6. Jennifer Bingham Hull, "Tonight's The Night (Maybe)," *Parenting,* June 2004, 73.
7. Valerie Davis Raskin, www.Dr-Valerie.com, 2003.
8. Downey, *Chicken Dance,* 194.

Chapter 9

1. Weiner-Davis, *Sex-Starved Marriage,* www.divorce busting.com.
2. Raskin, www.Dr-Valerie.com, 2003.
3. Ellen Kreidman, "Keep Marriage Hot," *Redbook,* February 2004.

About the Author

Lorilee Craker enjoyed researching this book with her husband, Doyle, who was a great asset to the process. She loves him dearly and, in fact, dedicated this tome to him (in code, using the cutesy nicknames they've had for each other since college days). Why then isn't the good man pictured here with Lorilee? Because, if you've read this book, you already know way too much about them both, that's why. Although, if you truly wish to see what the family looks like, take a gander at Lorilee's website, www.lorilee craker.com. There you'll also find photos of Jonah, now seven, and Ez the Pez, now four. And by the time this book comes out, Lorilee may even have photos posted of their new baby girl, Phoebe, adopted from Korea.

Since you now know pretty much all there is to know about Lorilee, she wishes you would e-mail her and tell her whether and how this book helped you get your mojo back. (Her e-mail address is also available at her Web site.)

Finally, if you've enjoyed this book, please check out Lorilee's other books including *A is for Adam: Biblical Baby Names; When the Belly Button Pops, the Baby's Done; O for a Thousand Nights to Sleep;* and *See How They Run.*

To learn more about WaterBrook Press and view
our catalog of products, log on to our Web site:
www.waterbrookpress.com

From Pregnancy to Potty Training—
Can't Miss Guides
for Your Baby's Early Years